At Piece with Time

A Woman's Journey Stitched in Cloth

Kristin C. Steiner & Diane C. Frankenberger

© 2003 Kristin C. Steiner and
Diane C. Frankenberger

EDITOR-IN-CHIEF: *Darra Williamson*
EDITOR: *Cyndy Lyle Rymer*
TECHNICAL EDITORS: *Sara Kate MacFarland and
Franki Kohler*
COPYEDITOR/PROOFREADER: *Linda D. Smith/
Carol Barrett*
COVER DESIGNER: *Christina Jarumay*
DESIGN DIRECTOR/BOOK DESIGNER: *Rose Sheifer*
ILLUSTRATOR: *Diane C. Frankenberger and
Tim Manibusan*
PRODUCTION ASSISTANT: *Kirstie L. McCormick*
PHOTOGRAPHY: *Sharon Risedorph and
Diane Pedersen except where noted*

Published by C&T Publishing, Inc., P.O. Box
1456, Lafayette, California 94549

FRONT COVER: *Photo by Garry Gay*
BACK COVER: *At Piece With Time Quilt,
Profound Pillow*

Library of Congress
Cataloging in Publication Division

Library of Congress Cataloging-in-Publication Data

Steiner, Kristin C.
   At piece with time: A woman's journey
stitched in cloth / Kristin C. Steiner ; illustrated by
Diane C. Frankenberger.
      p. cm.
   ISBN 1-57120-213-7 (paper trade)
   1. Patchwork--Patterns. 2. Quilting--Patterns.
I. Title.
   TT835.S726 2003
   746.46'041--dc21   2003002507

Printed in China
10 9 8 7 6 5 4 3 2 1

Childhood

Hopes and Dreams

Acceptance

Work

True Friends

Love

Motherhood

Safe Haven

Change

LOSS

Joy

Strength

Wisdom

Destination

CHILDHOOD

HOPES and DREAMS

ACCEPTANCE

Contents

WORK

MOTHERHOOD

TRUE FRIENDS

SAFE HAVEN

LOVE

CHANGE

JOY

LOSS

STRENGTH

WISDOM

DESTINATION

To the memory of my mother, Helen Thorpe Christensen. To her I owe my love of sewing. She nurtured my abilities to be a mother, yet always encouraged me to keep a "piece" of life set aside just for myself. She showed me what a strong wise woman is. I miss her greatly. And to the One above from Whom this deep yearning flows.

Kristin Steiner

This book is dedicated to the Lord, and to my mother, Suzanne Chase Frankenberger, who spoke to me a lot in one-liners. "Anything worth doing is worth doing well." Yes, Mom. And to women everywhere who teach just by being.

Diane Frankenberger

Acknowledgments

This is the book I've waited all my life to write. Its evolution, however, was an effort by a "dream" team. Diane's watercolor illustrations and dear stories transformed my words, adding life, richness, and texture. You are a priceless partner and I love working with you! Beth Calloway is my "better half," turning my quilt tops into quilts with the artistry of her machine quilting. Thank you, Beth, for the hours and all your caring. Rosie Sanford does some of the most beautiful appliqué you'll ever see. Thank you for stitching the Harvest Bouquet triangles and the little boys on the baby quilt for me. The experts at C&T encouraged me with words of experience and comforting thoughts of chocolate at just the right moments. A dream team indeed! Cathy Perlman inspired this title. When commenting on my love of appliqué she said, "Oh, you must be at peace with time!" Thank you, Cathy, for words that thrilled my spine. Having anything at all to say is due in large part to the many friends, teachers, and students who have touched my life. How can I thank you for all you've so generously shared? You have shaped and inspired me throughout the years. I feel you even now and am so very proud to travel, if for just a few miles, beside you. Patrick and Megan, thank you for asking once in a while how the book was going. You are two amazing young people and the world will be changed by your dreams! Bill, my one true love, walking with me every step of the way and believing in me has made me so much braver. Your understanding and tolerance through these many years have created the safe haven I needed to blossom. Thank you for this journey together, one of enduring commitment and constant growth.

Kristin Steiner

To my co-workers at People, Places, and Quilts: Jo Ann, Peggy, Enola, Suzanne, Tracy, Marianne, Vicki, Carolyn, Devy, Mary, Margaret, Louise, Kim, Barbara, Sue, and Sharon, who picked up the pieces of me and the store, making time for me to be at home working on this book as I struggled with a character defect of unrealistic time management goals! To my oldest daughter, Jerusha, the only one to see my work in progress and who said, "Hey Mom, this is really good." My other children, John, James, Julia, and daughter-in-law, Crystal, offered long-distance support just by believing in me and my efforts, no matter what. Thanks to all of the above for lighting my path, making the way smooth, and to the Lord and C&T for the path!

Diane Frankenberger

Welcome to the Journey

AN INTRODUCTION

I cut out my first quilt on the oak table my mother gave me when I married.

I did my best to follow the instructions printed in the thin *Quilter's Newsletter Magazine* from 1976, making my templates out of cereal cardboard and cutting each small diamond carefully by hand. Alone, with little frame of reference, I felt a strong connection to the quilt-makers who went before me. I could literally feel their presence guide my first wobbly stitches, encourage me when things got all tangled up, and urge me to enjoy the precious, almost sacred calm that comes from pushing a needle through scraps of fabric.

My love affair with fabric would see me through the demanding challenges of motherhood, would maintain my sanity through countless

Who am I? Where am I going? What am I doing? What's going on? Nothing. . .

moves across the country, would sustain my spirit as I lost dear family members, and would allow me to grow as a teacher and designer. This beautiful art form would, in fact, lead me on the most rewarding journey imaginable.

May I share a few of the twists and turns along the way? I blissfully quilted in isolation throughout most of the 1970s. It was a thrilling time. Every new technique seemed monumental and was often of my own devising. I loved my quilts and can't remember ever feeling self-conscious about them. I roared down my pathway full speed ahead.

In the 1980s, quiltmaking came into the spotlight with an ever-expanding smorgasbord of resources. It was a heady time, with much to learn and many things to try. I noticed, however, that I began to doubt myself as I allowed others to instruct me, tell me the rules, or say if my quilts were worthy or not. The road seemed increasingly filled with potholes and U-turns.

By the late 1990s I was in a quilting "funk." Piles of unfinished projects filled my workroom. I felt like a quilting "wanna be," trying every style, each new technique, but feeling more and more that I was losing myself. Where was the delight and full joy of creating quilts? My path seemed to peter out.

And then it happened, perhaps as an answer to my desperate frustration. An accident sharply impaired my thimble finger. Hard questions filled my mind as I sat stitchless for months. "Why do I quilt? What do my quilts say about me? What do I want to honor?" At last the answer came, glowing like a beacon in a shroud of bleakness. "If I am ever so blessed to quilt again, I vow to trust myself, to believe in my vision, and to create from my heart."

All quilts I have ever made can be measured by this fork in the road, before and after I began to trust myself. The ability to create from the heart is in each of us. Every quilter has a story to tell, a history to record, a unique journey to celebrate. *At Piece With Time* reminds you to make sweet "pieceful" time to set down in cloth your scrap bag of memories. Clear steps for creating a very personal album quilt are explained, resulting in

You can't anymore give away

something you ain't got than

you can come back from

someplace you ain't been. . .

the delight of documenting one's past, of finding one's voice, and the satisfying act of self-expression— a lasting legacy from a quilter's heart.

At Piece With Time is a feast for the senses. Designed with a beloved travel journal in mind, it is a collection of favorite souvenirs. Stunning watercolor illustrations by artist Diane Frankenberger grace every page. Recipes old and new are tucked in here and there to tantalize the taste buds. Inspiring quotes and heartwarming stories connect quilters across time. Most importantly, space is provided in the Travel Log for you to record your thoughts and feelings.

My most passionate wish is that you'll discover your wealth of creativity while on this journey. I hope that your eyes dance and sparkle as you share what is closest to your heart. Feel the joy that comes from honoring your vision, and trusting your instincts. This is an invitation to eloquently record the most important message of all: the record of your life stitched in cloth. Are you ready to begin?

Morning is welcome

to the industrious.

A Road Map and Directions

At Piece With Time, approximately 72'' x 86'' finished
Designed and pieced by Kristin Steiner; Harvest Bouquet triangles appliquéd by Rosie Sanford;
machine quilted by Beth Calloway

This is an album quilt (see page 9) designed to resemble a scrapbook. It's a place to collect and assemble the stories and

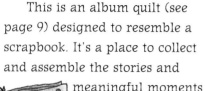

meaningful moments of our lives. Each block tells its own tale. It is also a medallion quilt, with a Blazing Star set on point at its center. Undulating appliqué triangles frame the center, with twelve traditional blocks surrounding all. Setting triangles and a series of borders complete the medallion.

To give this quilt a rich patina, use a wide variety of fabrics for the pieced blocks and their appliqués. To add depth to the quilt, use four slightly different background fabrics. We will call these Backgrounds 1, 2, 3, and 4. Using four different backgrounds gives our quilt the feeling of age, of chapters in a scrapbook filled with memories.

What is your background, darling?
I mean. . .where are you from?
Who are your people?

Southern Question

You know my mom has a quilt shop.
Oh yeah? Where?
In her closet!

Conversation

YARDAGE REQUIREMENTS

I recommend using 100% prewashed cotton fabrics. All requirements are based on 40''-wide fabric.

- Background 1, used in all pieced blocks: 2 yards medium
- Background 2, used in appliqué triangles: 1 yard medium light
- Background 3, used in center Blazing Star: fat quarter light
- Background 4, used as outer setting triangles: 1 yard medium dark
- Dark setting squares and triangles: 2 yards dark floral
- Fat quarters of assorted lights, mediums, and darks for pieced blocks and their appliqués
- Narrow frame border A and B: 2½ yards accent
- Final large border C: 3 yards dark floral
- Backing: 5½ yards
- Queen size batting: 90'' x 108''
- Binding: 1 yard for a 2½'' straight-grain double-fold binding

Please note there will be enough fabric left over from the Narrow Frame border if you choose to use it for the binding.

You're never gonna use that fabric! What are you getting it for? Just more stuff. Geez! I'm gonna go back here and sit down.

Husband in Quilt Shop

You do that dear. . .won't be but a minute. He's right you know. I'm not going to use it. It's too pretty bundled up this way. I'm going to put it around my sewing room to decorate.

Wife in Quilt Shop

General Directions
Tips for Successful Travel

Here are some tips for successful stitching.

1. Rotary cutting is fast, but work hard to keep it accurate. Double-check the position of your ruler before you cut. Measurements for rotary cutting include seam allowances. The following symbols denote cutting instructions:

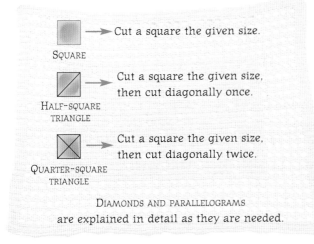

SQUARE → Cut a square the given size.

HALF-SQUARE TRIANGLE → Cut a square the given size, then cut diagonally once.

QUARTER-SQUARE TRIANGLE → Cut a square the given size, then cut diagonally twice.

DIAMONDS AND PARALLELOGRAMS
are explained in detail as they are needed.

2. The single most important challenge in making quilts is to stitch a consistent $1/4''$ seam allowance. Take some time to mark your sewing machine with an exact $1/4''$. Use masking tape or a layer of yellow sticky notes. A special $1/4''$ foot is also helpful. You need to be able to easily and consistently sew $1/4''$ from the edge of the fabric. Your care will pay off at your journey's end with blocks that fit together perfectly as you set your quilt together.

3. Pressing can really make a block look professional. Follow the pressing arrows in the diagrams and press as you go for crisp, well-behaved blocks.

4. Have fun! This is your journey. As you travel through each chapter, relax and enjoy the delightful process of stitching a part of yourself into every quilted detail.

You are a needle artist of the twenty-first century. Each careful decision, every well-placed stitch, and the attention given to accuracy and precision all combine to reflect your skilled craftsmanship. These are things to be proud of. Take your time and do your best work. The beauty of your efforts will be your lasting reward.

A good beginning makes a good ending.

Dreamy Appliqué
Kristi's Tips for Stitching Flawlessly

Appliqué is such a gentle art. It is handwork supreme! Many of us hunger for a way to slow down and unwind. Hand appliqué affords us just this opportunity. Snuggle up in your favorite chair as I share more than 25 years of appliqué tips guaranteed to help you navigate the challenges of hand appliqué.

TOOLS

Thread: Use the finest thread available. I love Mettler 100% cotton 60-weight embroidery thread, or its cousin, the 50-weight silk finish. These threads are widely available in quilt stores. They come in a million colors and stand up beautifully to the repeated action of the

Today is yesterday's pupil.

appliqué stitch. Silk thread by YLI is also wonderful. When choosing thread, try to match the color of the piece you are appliquéing as closely as possible. If you are uncertain, choose a darker or duller color. You are looking for a "shy" thread that will retire quietly into your stitching. No "loud mouth" threads allowed here!

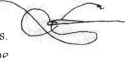

Needles: There is no substitute for a thin needle. I adore #12 John James sharp needles. Although threading such a tiny needle eye can be daunting, I try to think of it this way: Threading a large-eyed needle is easy for one minute, but difficult to maneuver for the remainder of the stitching time. Threading a small-eyed needle is difficult for one minute, but totally dreamy for each and every stitch. You choose.

Needle threader: If you choose the small #12 needles, you will definitely want a fine needle threader. My favorite is the heart-shaped threader by Clover.

Fine silk pins: These make positioning each appliqué piece easy and accurate.

Stiletto: Turning sharp curves and precise points is easier if you have a stiletto at hand. Try the brass ones available at quilt shops, or a simple toothpick from your pantry.

Sharp embroidery scissors: Clipping curves, cutting out small pieces, and ending threads is a breeze with small, sharp scissors.

Tracing paper: A tablet of 14'' x 17'' tracing paper allows you to make overlays for all appliqué projects shown in this book.

Black .01 Pigma pen: Use this pen for marking your freezer-paper templates and tracing-paper overlays. It produces a clear, fine line and is smudge free.

Freezer paper: I suggest you use freezer paper for all your appliqué templates.

PREPARATION FOR APPLIQUÉ

I recommend a system of appliqué based on a tracing paper overlay, freezer-paper templates, and a needle-turn technique. A bit of preparation is necessary to set up this very workable system in which no pencil marks are used.

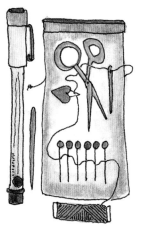

1. Place guideline markings on your background. These mark the center of your work. For full appliqué backgrounds like those used for the sweet children in the *Ring Around the Rosy Baby Quilt*, fold the background in half and then into quarters to establish markings. Crease firmly with an iron. To preserve the creases, baste along each one with a large basting stitch using a contrasting thread.

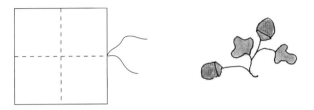

   For appliqué done on the pieced blocks, you can often use the intersections or seamlines to guide the placement of the appliqué. If necessary, you may crease an area in half and then in quarters to help center your design.

2. Create a tracing paper overlay. This is a paper "positioning guide" that helps you correctly place each appliqué on your background. For larger appliqués like those in the Harvest Bouquet triangles or the baby quilt, use a full sheet of your 14''x 17'' tracing paper. Fold it in half and then in quarters. Use a straight edge and your Pigma pen to mark long slash lines along these crease lines. You now have guidelines marking the center of your tracing paper overlay.

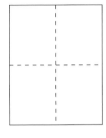

   Place tracing paper over your appliqué pattern, aligning all guideline markings. Trace the pattern onto paper. You now have the complete pattern information transferred to your tracing paper overlay.

   For appliqué on the pieced blocks, simply copy the guidelines as well as the appliqué pattern onto a small piece of tracing paper.

3. Create templates by tracing each shape from your pattern onto the dull side of a piece of freezer paper with a Pigma pen. If a shape is overlapped by a future piece, add an appropriate extension to the freezer-paper template. Indicate this extension with a dotted line and use small slashes to mark where the two pieces lock up.

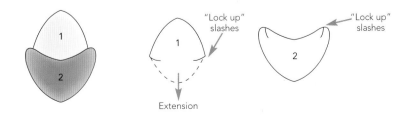

4. Cut out templates on the drawn line. Iron the shiny side of the freezer paper to the right side of your fabric.

5. Seam allowances are generally a scant ¹/4''. One of my best secrets is a small seam allowance. The smaller the piece, the smaller your seam allowance should be. Just be sure your seam allowances are consistent.

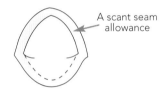

A scant seam allowance

6. Using your tracing paper overlay, position your first piece onto your background. Pin in place by pinning into the seam allowance. This causes the least disturbance to the correct position of your appliqué. Baste with large stitches through freezer paper, appliqué, and background. Baste inside the appliqué, at least ¹/4'' away from the outside edge. This allows you to turn under the seam allowance without hitting your basting stitches.

Place pin in seam allowance, then baste.

THE APPLIQUÉ STITCH

All of your preparation work is complete! Let's get to the delicious work of doing the actual appliqué stitch.

1. Thread your needle with about 15" of thread that closely matches your appliqué piece.

2. Begin by using your needle to turn your seam allowance under the guiding edge of your freezer-paper template. This fold should "shadow" just a bit beyond the template, resulting in a smooth, even margin. Use your needle to smooth out any gathers. Your needle is your best tool here. Use it to swoop along the inside of the stitching edges and set the fold.

Needle-turn for a smooth margin.

3. My favorite appliqué stitch is the straightforward tack stitch. Begin your stitching by hiding your knot on the back of the background fabric. Come up through all layers into the edge of your fold.

4. Go down into the background only, exactly below your last stitch. This stitch should be very straight and short, thus its name, tack stitch.

5. Now take a stitch along the back, moving ahead about ¹⁄₁₆". Come up again into the edge of your fold. Repeat the above steps, trying to keep your stitches as small and invisible as possible.

6. Snuggle your stitches about every fifth stitch or so to fully embed them in your appliqué.

7. Don't stitch what you don't see. The extensions you added when you made your template are usually not stitched down.

8. Live in the moment! The most successful appliqué is done a tiny bit at a time. This helps avoid the pesky gathers that make unsightly points and peaks at the edge of the appliqué. Use your needle often to swoop, ensuring a smooth, even fold. Smooth, even, and beautiful are the results of your careful work.

He who rides slowly gets just as far, only it takes a little longer.

EMERGENCY AID FOR PROBLEM APPLIQUÉ SHAPES

There are three "roadblocks" for most appliquérs. Many of us have trouble stitching sharp leaf points, smooth outside curves, and deep dips. With a few well-placed hints, I know you will maneuver these sticky areas with skill.

SHARP LEAF POINTS

1. I recommend starting your leaf at the stem end—the point where the leaf connects to a vine or stem. Begin your appliqué here, turning under the seam allowance and placing your first stitch at the very tip of the leaf.

2. Stitch as usual, moving up to the outer point of the leaf.

Start stitching at a stem end.

3. Look closely at the leaf point. If there is *excess* seam allowance extending from the seam you've just completed, trim it now. This eliminates as much bulk as possible from this very narrow area.

Trim

4. Use your needle to prick the tip of the leaf point seam allowance and slowly draw it down and under the appliqué shape. You want this tip to fold under flat. You can do it! Simply avoid any action that results in a bunched wad of seam allowance beneath the point.

Anchor stitch

5. Pull your appliqué thread to clearly define the leaf point. Now place an anchoring stitch at the point.

6. Beautiful! Now continue down the second side of the leaf. Stop 1/4" before the stem end. With your needle, draw in the last of your seam allowance, smoothing the fold with your needle. Continue stitching until you meet your initial stitch. Great job!

CURVES

The secret for stitching smooth curves is to slow down. It's very similar to driving a car in the mountains. You slow down for steep curves, right? This applies to appliqué as well. The sharper the curve, the more you will want to emphasize this technique.

1. Fold under just a tiny bit of seam allowance. Swoop with your needle to smooth out any puckers or gathers.

2. Take just one or two stitches.

3. Fold under a tiny bit more seam allowance. Stitch.

4. Think of yourself as a sculptor. You are forming the smooth rounded curves tiny bit by tiny bit. This works for any curve and for circles of all sizes.

Slow down and turn under just a tiny bit of seam allowance.

DEEP DIPS

Dips and deep valleys are an integral part of appliqué. Try these easy steps to handle this challenge.

1. Stitch to 1/4" from your dip.

2. Clip the dip, stopping two threads shy of the freezer paper.

Clip

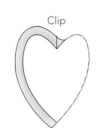

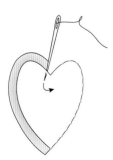

Swoop the seam allowance under with your needle.

3. Now jump ahead to the opposite side of the dip. With your needle, set your fold and swoop the seam allowance under all the way through the dip, continuing on to meet your last stitch. This swooping action should pull under the area you've clipped, resulting in a small but definite fold.

4. Resume stitching up to the deepest part of the dip. Here is where the pesky "whisker" lives, the result of your clip. At this point, it is most effective to break your appliqué stitch into two parts. Stab down into your background with the first part of your stitch. Finally, stab back up into the edge of the fold with the second part of your stitch. Repeat if necessary until you feel you've moved beyond the clip of the dip. This allows you to carefully tack down the whisker without whip stitching it down. Dreamy!

A little too late

is much too late.

A Travel Journal
A Record of Your Heart's Desires

For any serious traveler, a map is vital. Roads, points of interest, probable congestion, and natural features are clearly laid out on the surface of a map. Consulting this helpful tool can make the choice of side trips, detours, and rest stops more informed.

As voyagers of the heart, we too need a map. That's what a journal is. . .a record and a compass for this wild and winding trek we are on. Some of us are drawn to the habit of writing every day. Others are nervous and shy. Rest assured, this book is for your eyes only. The simple act of putting pen to paper can be a powerful catalyst for the ideas and understanding fermenting inside each of us. We can relax and trust the process. Creating a special time each morning or evening to "spill our hearts" on the page provides a way to slow down time, to embrace the quiet, and to at last listen to the whispers of our souls. Won't you join me in this record of the heart?

WHAT YOU'LL NEED

A journal with a plain cover: Take your time to search out a journal perfectly suited to you. Do you like spirals or bound books; big sketchbooks or small slender volumes? Please yourself.

- Two 5'' squares fabric, 1 for the small heart A, and 1 for its lining
- Two 7'' squares fabric, 1 for the large heart B, and 1 for its lining
- An old button, lace, ribbon, or charms to add your personal touch to this cover
- Glue: I use Aleene's Tacky Glue.

A note about the fabric: I adore collecting and using decorator-weight fabric for many of my projects. The sturdy weight means no need to interface and the colors are to die for! I can't resist them for the hearts. I use regular cotton-weight fabrics for the linings.

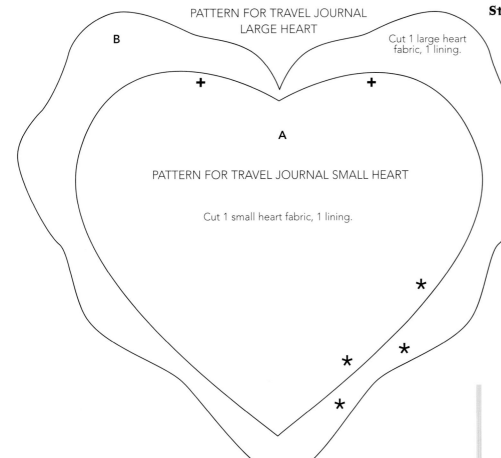

PATTERN FOR TRAVEL JOURNAL
LARGE HEART

B

Cut 1 large heart
fabric, 1 lining.

+   +

A

PATTERN FOR TRAVEL JOURNAL SMALL HEART

Cut 1 small heart fabric, 1 lining.

Step 5: Spread glue evenly on the backside of the large heart. Position it on your journal cover. Placing a heavy book on the heart "sandwich" will help it firmly adhere to the cover. Now add a touch of magic to your journal by putting a meaningful talisman in the pocket. You could choose a charm, a piece of family jewelry, a favorite quote rolled up like a little scroll. . . anything you choose to inspire this record of your heart!

Step 1: Use pattern piece A to cut 1 small heart and 1 small heart lining. Place right sides together and stitch using a $1/4''$ seam. Leave open for turning between *s. Turn right side out, press well and slipstitch opening closed.

Step 2: Sew a lovely button or medallion of lace on the finished small heart. Set aside.

Step 3: Use pattern piece B to cut 1 large heart and 1 large heart lining. Sew as you did for the small heart. You will need to clip the many curves on this heart to maintain the scalloped effect. Turn, press, and stitch opening closed.

Step 4: Center small heart on top of the large heart. Topstitch around the small heart, starting and stopping at +. This creates the opening of a secret pocket.

There was an old woman
tossed up in a basket nineteen
times as high as the moon,
And where she was going, I
couldn't but ask it, for in her
hand she carried a broom.
"Old woman, old woman, old
woman," quoth I, "Oh whither,
O whither, O whither so high?"
"To sweep the cobwebs out
of the sky!"
"Shall I go with thee?"
"Ay, by and by."

Mother Goose

Ring Around the Rosy

Ask anyone about her childhood and you'll undoubtedly see eyes twinkling. Hours of play with paint, mud, water, and dolls are remembered with tender fondness. Games and contests were devised with neighborhood friends and lasted deep into the night. With intense absorption, we dedicated ourselves to our passions. Details of nature intrigued us, tempting us to experiment and question. We made plans, tried them out, were often surprised by the outcome, but always delighted with the process. Our rhythms were a perfect tempo as we lived true to our own nature, pleasing only ourselves.

Ready or not, here I come!

Traversing the territory of passage to adulthood, we often return to these seeds of childhood, planted so long ago. In finding our distinctive path, we call on the grounding of our past to center and focus us. We reclaim our deepest passions as the guiding force that shapes our contributions to the world. We discover once again the power and creativity of play, experimentation, and of pleasing ourselves. The child within remembers what it is like to try, to fall, to try again as seeds of talent sprout and valiantly flower. In making the journey toward our beautiful, most-magnificent selves, we circle around again, like the game Ring Around the Rosy, back to the truths of our youth. There lie the treasures of our deepest heart, the unfailing guideposts to our surest path.

Childhood

Our journey begins in the rich garden of childhood. Here in the fertile soil of youth, seeds of our potential are planted. Nurtured by hours of play, close observation, and experimenting; warmed by passionate absorption in our favorite things; strengthened by standing up and falling down, then standing up once and for all, these dear seeds sprout, forming the roots of who we are today.

TRAVEL LOG

I just can't help it! Every time I look at the happy clumps of daisies in my spring garden, I giggle. They are so simple and pure, the epitome of the innocence they symbolize. Reflecting on your childhood, what were your favorite things, colors, or activities? Can you trace their presence in your life today? Jot some notes here.

He loves me...
He Loves me
He Loves me Not
He Loves Me!

_____

_____

Ring Around the Rosy

10'' finished

Follow the piecing order of this carefully and you won't get lost.

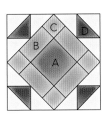

A	4''		→	Cut 1 medium
B	4'' x 2¼''		→	Cut 4 floral
C	2¼''		→	Cut 4 accent
D	3⅜''		→	Cut 2 dark
E 3⅜''			→	6 Background 1

light

When I was ten, my best friends were twins, Denise and Debbie. I adored them. I took all my playthings in a wagon to go play, dolls and kitchen stuff. I didn't like to play at their house, though; their mom was so mean. I didn't like her one bit, but I loved her daughters. MG

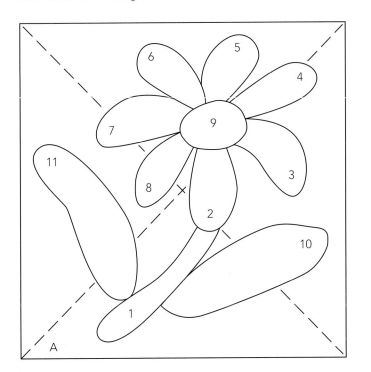

APPLIQUÉ
PATTERN FOR
DAISY

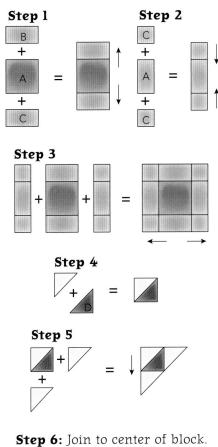

Step 1

Step 2

Step 3

Step 4

Step 5

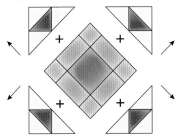

Step 6: Join to center of block.

Here's a great hint when lining up this triangle unit with the block center. Use a ruler to measure in ⅜'' from the tips of the long side of each triangle unit. Make a small mark on the wrong side of the fabric. We'll call this a matching mark. Match this mark to the raw edge of the center square. The result should be equal bunny ears on each side of the square. So easy and so helpful!

Step 7: Make a tracing paper overlay for the daisy. Appliqué to center A. HOORAY!

Ring Around the Rosy Baby Quilt

40'' x 40''

Designed by Kristin Steiner, appliquéd by Rosie Sanford

Four little children hold hands with daisy "stars" in this sweet baby quilt. I did my entire appliqué by hand, but feel free to use your favorite fusible web and machine stitching to make this childproof. Change the colors and make it more appropriate for a boy, use just girls and you have a cute tea party quilt, or add machine embroidery details to each of the pieced block centers. I just know the possibilities are dancing in your head.

YARDAGE REQUIREMENTS

- ¾ yard background fabric for little girls appliqué
- ¾ yard coordinating background fabric for little boys appliqué
- Fat quarters or scraps for the children's clothes
- Fat quarter flesh color for faces, arms, and legs
- Fat quarter white for daisy stars
- Large scrap yellow for daisy star centers
- Fat quarters or scraps for the 4 pieced blocks
- 1 yard border fabric
- 1½ yards backing fabric
- Crib size batting: 45'' x 60''
- ¾ yard binding fabric

We loved to put "nice" bugs on our arms. They tickled us as they crawled.

DCF

CUTTING RECIPE

BACKGROUNDS FOR APPLIQUÉD CHILDREN

10'' finished

Cut two 12'' squares from each girl and boy background fabric. These are oversized and will be trued up once the appliqué is complete.

BORDERS

Cut 4 rectangles 10½'' x 20½''.

BINDING

Cut 5 strips 2½'' x fabric width.

RING AROUND THE ROSY BLOCKS

10'' finished. Make 4 blocks.

For each block cut:

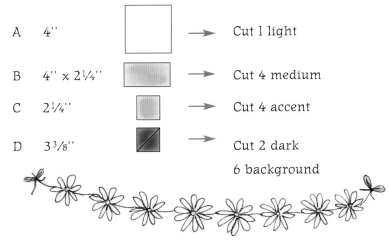

A	4''	→ Cut 1 light
B	4'' x 2¼''	→ Cut 4 medium
C	2¼''	→ Cut 4 accent
D	3⅜''	→ Cut 2 dark
		6 background

Step 1: Hand appliqué the children.
Prepare each of the 4 background squares with basted guidelines as shown on page 11. Make tracing paper overlay for girl and for boy. Appliqué the children following the easy numbering sequence given on each appliqué piece.

Step 2: Square up each of the 4 appliquéd blocks using the method described on page 66. True up to 10½'' unfinished.

Step 3: Sew the appliqué blocks together. Position a daisy star between each child's hands. The daisy will fall along the block seamline. Stitch. Set aside.

Step 4: Construct each of the 4 pieced blocks using the directions on page 17.

Step 5: Assemble the quilt top.

Step 6: Baste and quilt the baby quilt by hand or machine. Bind with a 2½'' double-fold straight-grain binding. Now christen your quilt with a tea party and your favorite childhood story. Sweet dreams!

Have you ever heard of the
Sugar-Plum Tree?
'Tis a marvel of great renown!
It blooms on the shore
of the Lollypop Sea
In the garden of
Shut Eye Town;
The fruit that it bears is so
wondrously sweet
(as those that have
tasted it say)
That good little children
have only to eat
Of that fruit to be
happy next day. . .

Eugene Field

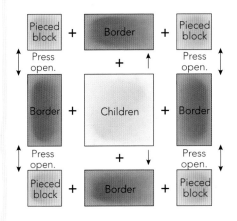

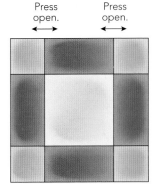

GIRL APPLIQUÉ PATTERN FOR
RING AROUND THE ROSY BABY QUILT

Enlarge by 200%.

APPLIQUÉ PATTERN FOR DAISY STAR
RING AROUND THE ROSY BABY QUILT

BOY APPLIQUÉ PATTERN FOR
RING AROUND THE ROSY BABY QUILT

Enlarge by 200%.

As a child I was safe. Not like
today. I would play in a
playground blocks from home.
We all knew our mothers' horns.
When it was lunchtime, our
mothers would go out to the
carport, lean into the car, and
beep the horn. Mom wasn't
gonna get in the car and come
get me. She just blew the horn.
MG

Twinkling Star

Growing up in the wilds of a ranch in Colorado, I had vast amounts of time to dream. I remember always

being the heroine, the one who took charge and saved the day, the smart one, the strong one, the beautiful one. I never could settle for just "one" dream, such as growing up to be a doctor or anything else so specific. No, the roles were many and excitingly varied to provide the most entertainment.

Reflecting back, what strikes me most is the enormous potential I allowed myself. Doubts about my ability and fears of lack of talent or strength never entered my imaginings. Boundaries and limits were not a part of my dreams. A seed, a nugget, a small acorn of potential burned as bright as any twinkling star inside my young heart.

It seems much of our journey into womanhood is about the losing, then the regaining, of this absolute belief in "self." The losing begins when we start looking outside ourselves, thinking others are more capable, talented, or beautiful. College, first jobs, rocky relationships, new experiences handled less than perfectly all do their work—slowly chipping away at the fierce dreams we had. Bump, bump, bump; the path gets a bit rocky here, the acorn lies dormant, and the star faintly glimmers.

Hopes and Dreams

"Twinkle, twinkle, little star. . ." Aren't those words part of every childhood? Didn't each of us, in the safety of our own backyard, spend endless summer evenings simply staring into the deep night sky, dreaming? Dreams were the precious jewels of our youth where anything seemed possible.

TRAVEL LOG

Throughout the ages, stars have meant "Divine guidance." Looking up to the heavens at night, it's easy to feel stellar encouragement to stay on the path to our truest self. Our pattern for Twinkling Star can serve as a record of our amazing progress. Perhaps when stitching the small corner stars we can celebrate our finest triumphs or simple truths that shine for us no matter what happens along our journey. The acorn in the center of the block is our ripening potential. Just think of the strong, sturdy oak tree residing inside. Why don't you take a moment to list your thoughts about dreams of youth, present hopes, and your "taproot" of resilience?

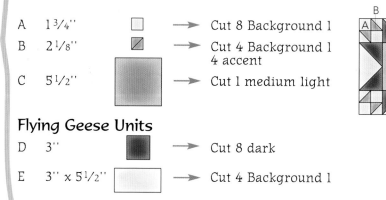

MY HOPES, DREAMS & STRENGTHS

Twinkle, twinkle, little star, How I wonder what you are! Up above the world so high, like a diamond in the sky. Twinkle, twinkle, little star, How I wonder what you are!

From "The Star" by Ann & Jane Taylor

If you don't know where you're going, any road will do.

Gentle whispers, soft nudges, and growing to a "certain age" eventually allow the light of renewed faith to shine on the little acorn buried deep within ourselves. Time and experience on the road help us see that our talents and skills are perfectly suited for important, meaningful work. Our ability to endure frustration, failure, and disappointment helps us creatively find new ways of thinking. We build on our successes, knowing we are strong and resourceful. We dare to dream BIG again as we gaze at the twinkling stars above. We realize something so very beautiful. Gentle guidance assures us that we do in fact have all we'll ever need, shining brightly within our perfectly powerful acorn-self.

Twinkling Star

10" finished

This is a fun star to piece. The challenge is to accurately stitch the tiny corner triangles. Just watch your seam allowance, perhaps making it one or two threads shy of $1/4$". Press well following the arrows and your star will brightly shine.

CUTTING RECIPE

A	$1^3/4$"	☐	→	Cut 8 Background 1
B	$2^1/8$"	◨	→	Cut 4 Background 1 4 accent
C	$5^1/2$"	▨	→	Cut 1 medium light

Flying Geese Units

D	3"	■	→	Cut 8 dark
E	3" x $5^1/2$"	☐	→	Cut 4 Background 1

Step 1: Make the Flying Geese units using this precise and easy method. Draw a pencil line diagonally from corner to corner on the wrong side of all D squares.

Place one D on the left-hand corner of one E, right sides together. Stitch, aiming your needle one thread to the left of the line. (This allows for the seam when pressing. You may want to "test drive" once to get just the right aim!) Now press D open, lining up the raw edges with the edges of E. Trim excess fabric to 1/4''.

Place a second D on the right-hand corner of E. Stitch, aiming just one thread to the right of the line this time. Open to check your accuracy, press, and trim. There you have it—a perfect Flying Geese unit resulting in one set of star points. Repeat to total 4 geese.

Step 2: Make 8.

Step 3: Make 4. A + B =

Step 4: Make 4. Press open.

Shoot for the moon! If you miss, you'll be among the stars.

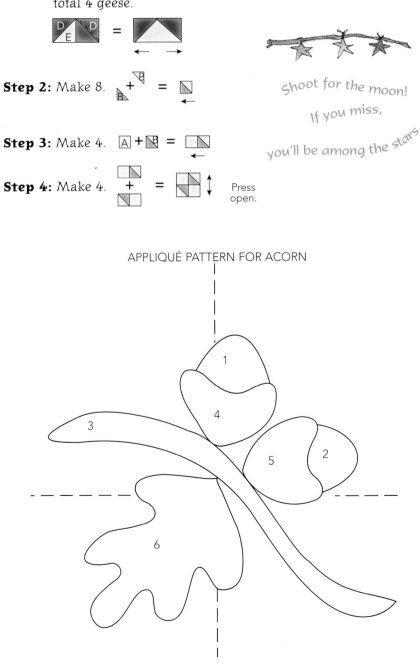

APPLIQUÉ PATTERN FOR ACORN

. . . I still have a dream. It is a dream deeply rooted in the American dream. I have a dream that one day this nation will rise up and live out the true meaning of its creed: "We hold these truths to be self evident: that all men are created equal.". . . I have a dream that my four children will one day live in a nation where they will not be judged by the color of their skin but by the content of their character. I have a dream today. . . I have a dream that one day, every valley shall be exalted, every hill and mountain shall be made low, the rough places will be made plain and the crooked places will be made straight. . . this is the hope. This is the faith. . . free at last!

  Martin Luther King, Jr.

Step 5: Assemble the rows.

Rows 1 and 3

Row 2

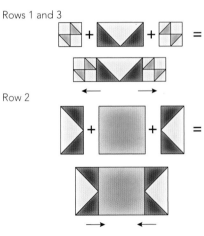

Step 6: Join the rows, carefully matching intersections.

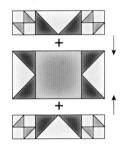

Step 7: Make a tracing paper overlay for the acorn appliqué. Stitch acorns and leaf to center C. Beautiful!

Grandmother's Favorite

A magical "grandmother vision" saw the possibilities and potential within our little girl selves. She saw our fascination with needle and thread and gladly encouraged us through our first clumsy stitches. She listened repeatedly to our first songs on the piano and asked for more. She praised our efforts in all things, whether it was gardening, reading, knitting, or baking. "You can do it, Buttercup!" were the words she spoke with enough conviction to hold and guide us through the unknown years ahead.

Her patient listening made us feel we always mattered. Time seemed endless as we sat together in her humble kitchen over lemonade and cookies. There, in the safety of her non-judgmental environment, we could spill out our hearts. We could bitterly complain about sibling injustices, knowing she would never take sides. We could gush with excitement over the new friendships we'd made, feeling her support and happiness for us. We dared to explore our first probings into a philosophy of life, trusting her to temper our ideas with her own gentle observations of wisdom and experience

Her patience, listening, understanding, and vision—all woven together effortlessly—formed the greatest covering any of us could receive, a soft nurturing blanket of complete acceptance. Is it any wonder we felt we were Grandmother's Favorite?

Acceptance

Her name was Grammy, Muzzy, Mimi, Nana, Lola, or just plain Grandma. Many of us grew up knowing at least one grandmother. Some were "fun" while others were "fussy." Some felt the need to correct and admonish, while others were immediate cohorts in all sorts of schemes and adventures. Our relationship with a favorite grandmother blessed us with the rarest kind of love: unconditional love.

She believed in me until I could believe in myself. KCS

TRAVEL LOG

What I remember most are my Muzzy's eyes. They were beautiful Scandinavian blue eyes, like the soft blue in the center of this block. In an ironic twist of fate, glaucoma robbed her of sight, leaving her in the darkness of midnight blue for most of my childhood. She never let her disability interfere with the things she loved: living independently, baking her famous weekly bread, playing the piano every day. What are your memories of your treasured grandmother?

We owe our grandmothers such gratitude for seeing our "gold" hidden deep beneath the rough exterior of our childishness. The buttercup symbolizes this gift with little leaf "wings" ready to help us fly.

Grandmother's Favorite
10" finished

Piecing the four small B triangles together carefully is important in this block. Perhaps you would like to pick colors that remind you of your grandmother's dresses, her eyes, or her home.

CUTTING RECIPE

NOT A MEASURE OF YOUR WORTH

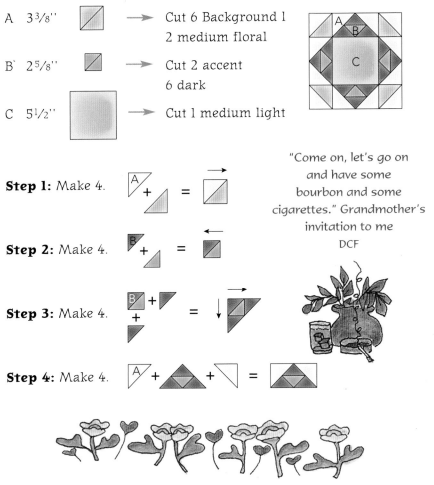

A $3\frac{3}{8}$" → Cut 6 Background
2 medium floral

B $2\frac{5}{8}$" → Cut 2 accent
6 dark

C $5\frac{1}{2}$" → Cut 1 medium light

Step 1: Make 4.

Step 2: Make 4.

Step 3: Make 4.

Step 4: Make 4.

"Come on, let's go on and have some bourbon and some cigarettes." Grandmother's invitation to me
DCF

Lord, make us instruments of your peace. Where there is hatred, let us sow love; where there is injury, pardon; where there is despair, hope; where there is darkness, light; where there is sadness, joy. Grant that we may not so much seek to be consoled as to console; to be understood as to understand; to be loved as to love. For it is in giving that we receive; it is in pardoning that we are pardoned; and it is in dying that we are born to eternal life.

Prayer of St. Francis of Assisi

Hey! I'm home!

Child

Child, what in the heck
have you done to your hair?
It looks just awful!

Mother

Mother, I think it looks cute!

Grandmother

Once, before there were too
many cars on the roads where
my grandmother lived, she had
asked my mother to drive her
somewhere. Not a patient
person, when they came to a red
light my grandmother instructed
my mother to "just go on!
Nobody's coming!"

DCF

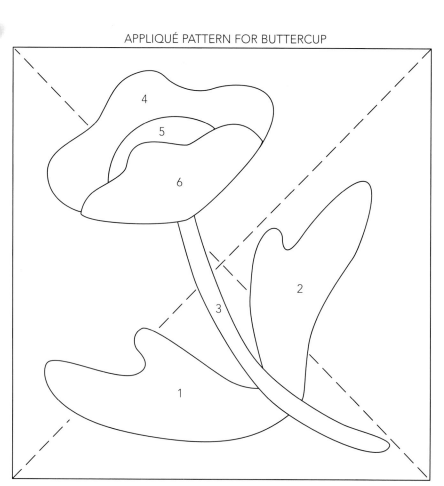

Step 5: Assemble the rows.

Rows 1 and 3

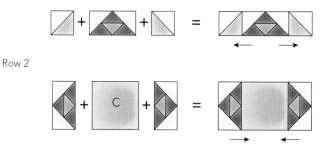

Row 2

Step 6: Join the rows, carefully matching intersections.

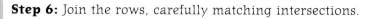

Press both
seams open.

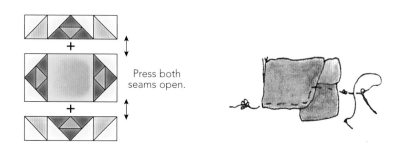

Step 7: Make a tracing paper overlay for the buttercup appliqué.
Stitch in the center of C. Grandmother would love it!

My First Quilt and Baby Doll

Designed and told by Diane Frankenberger

WHAT YOU NEED FOR DOLL, DOLL'S DRESS, AND DIAPER

- ⅓ yard solid-colored fabric for body (flannel is great...so soft!)
- Fat quarter print for doll dress
- Fat quarter white for diaper
- 6'' x 3'' scrap fabric for hair; should be reversible
- Embroidery floss for stitching face, heart, and dress decoration
- One small bag polyfil
- 2 small safety pins to pin diaper on
- Freezer paper for templates

SUGGESTIONS

Copy all pattern pieces onto freezer paper. Patterns do not include seam allowance, so the drawn line is your stitching line! Transfer the embroidery for face and dress design using a lightbox or window. Easy!

My doll's name is Lily Rose Violet May. What's yours?

Annie was the name of my favorite doll, the only doll I remember from my early childhood. She had a cloth body, but her hands, face, and feet were hard; not plastic, but not porcelain either. I loved her. She was a comfort. My mother gave her away one day with other childhood treasures she thought I was finished with. I wasn't. Here is a softer version of Annie.

Baby Doll
16'' tall

CUTTING RECIPE FOR BABY DOLL, DRESS, AND DIAPER

From solid-colored body fabric:
- Cut 1 face lining.
- Cut 2 doll bodies.
- Cut 4 legs.
- Cut 4 arms.

From hair fabric:
- Cut 1.

From diaper fabric:
- Cut 2.

From dress fabric:
- Cut 1 following cutting diagram carefully!

Step 1: Place face lining on wrong side of doll's face. This piece just keeps the back of your embroidery stitches from showing through on the right side of the face. Embroider face. Also embroider heart on doll body.

Step 2: Position hair on right side front of doll's body at hair line. Place doll back right sides together with doll front. Stitch, leaving openings for arms and legs. Turn right side out and stuff. Snip doll's hair every half inch or so. Style to your liking. Add a bow.

Step 3: Sew arms and legs. Stuff well.

Step 4: Turn in 1/4'' on body arm and leg openings. Insert stuffed arms and legs. Stitch across body to close. Admire your baby doll!

DIAPER

Step 1: Place right sides together. Stitch, leaving a small opening.

Step 2: Turn right side out. Slipstitch opening closed.

Step 3: Small safety pins secure the diaper.

DRESS

Step 1: Follow cutting diagram to cut out dress.

Step 2: Hem sleeve edge by turning under 1/8'' twice. Stitch.

Step 3: Hem neck edge by turning under 1/8'' twice. Stitch.

Step 4: Embroider design on dress front using 3 strands of floss and your favorite embroidery stitches.

Step 5: Open dress out flat. Fold at shoulders with right sides together. Stitch each side of dress from sleeve edge to bottom of dress.

Step 6: Hem bottom edge of dress by turning under 1/4'' twice. Stitch.

Step 7: To close dress at the neckline, attach a 6-strand piece of floss to each side of back neck to be used as ties. Now diaper, dress, and hug this baby doll!

Baby Doll Quilt
13 1/2'' x 13 1/2'' finished

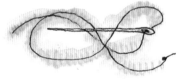

This quilt is perfect for a first stitching project. What fun to share it with a young quilter. Be sure to stop often for cookies and lemonade. Yummy!

WHAT YOU NEED

- Fat quarter or several scraps light fabric for squares
- Fat quarter or several scraps dark fabric for squares
- 1/4 yard or 4 strips floral fabric for border
- 15'' square of batting
- 18'' square of backing that coordinates with quilt top

CUTTING RECIPE

- From light fabric: Cut 32 squares 1 3/4'' x 1 3/4''.
- From dark fabric: Cut 32 squares 1 3/4'' x 1 3/4''.
- From border fabric: Cut 4 strips 2 1/4'' x 14''.

Step 1: Using 2 light and 2 dark fabrics, make 16 Four-Patch  blocks. Press toward the dark fabric.

Step 2: Join these into 4 rows, each containing 4 Four-Patch blocks. Press seams of alternating rows in opposite directions.

Step 3: Sew the 4 rows together to form quilt top. Press seams down.

Step 4: Sew border strips around quilt top in a Log Cabin fashion. Trim to fit. Press toward borders.

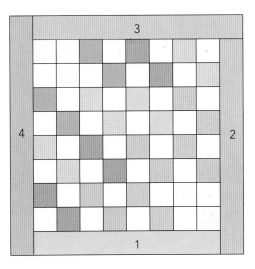

Step 5: Layer quilt backing right side down, then batting, and finally the quilt top. Trim quilt backing 1½'' larger than quilt top on all 4 sides. Baste or pin layers together. Quilt or hand tie.

Step 6: Bind your quilt by bringing the backing over to the front. Fold under binding edge ¼'', one side at a time. Whipstitch in place. Cover your baby doll. So sweet!

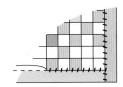

That's no fair. I'm not gonna play with you anymore! I'm going home. I'm gonna get a Popsicle and you can't have one! So there! Neener neener neener!

Childhood problem solving

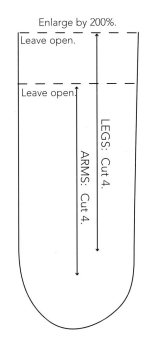

Enlarge by 200%.

Leave open.

Leave open.

LEGS: Cut 4.

ARMS: Cut 4.

PATTERN FOR DOLL BABY

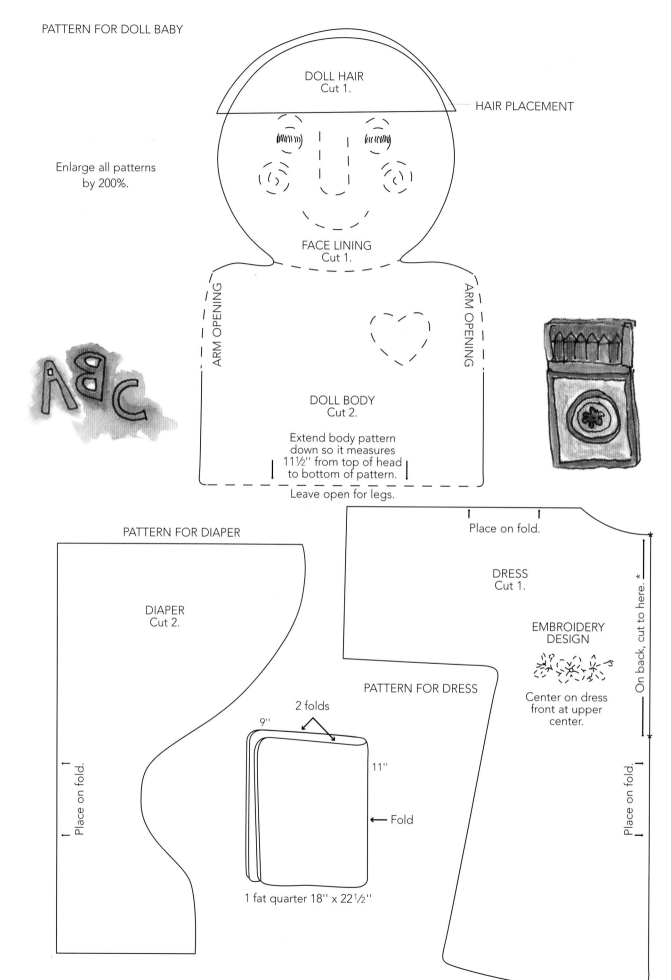

Enlarge all patterns
by 200%.

DOLL HAIR
Cut 1.

HAIR PLACEMENT

FACE LINING
Cut 1.

ARM OPENING

ARM OPENING

DOLL BODY
Cut 2.

Extend body pattern
down so it measures
11½'' from top of head
to bottom of pattern.

Leave open for legs.

PATTERN FOR DIAPER

DIAPER
Cut 2.

Place on fold.

Place on fold.

DRESS
Cut 1.

EMBROIDERY
DESIGN

Center on dress
front at upper
center.

On back, cut to here.

Place on fold.

PATTERN FOR DRESS

2 folds

9''

11''

← Fold

1 fat quarter 18'' x 22½''

Friendship Star

Making quilts is often a communal act. Gathering over a quilt frame or working on our own projects at a quilting bee, we join together with "sisters" who share our delight in stitching, our fascination with color, and our desire to create something out of cloth. The thrill of new  patterns, the excitement of a finished quilt, the adventure of attending a symposium or workshop together are threads that bind our hearts. Tentative at first, they grow stronger with each shared experience, weaving our souls together in meaningful connections.

The Friendship Star so aptly represents our feelings about good friends. Much more than a mere acquaintance, each beloved friend shines in a unique way, adding her special touch to our lives. We know instantly which friend can do the hard math required to figure out yardage for our quilts, and who we can consult with questions about design. We know who can draw up a template or a flower. We likewise know who to turn to for advice with teenagers, worries over aging parents, the loss of a loved one, or an illness of our own. True friends join us on our journey, supporting us through times of disappointment and of celebration, accepting us as we are, sharing strengths and talents, and always, always believing deeply in us. The lovely geranium in our block represents true friendship as it blossoms to color and enrich our path.

I loved my aunts. I remember visiting them in a nursing home: Emma, Edith, and Lula Mae. Seems like each one had something happen: cancer, broken hip, something, and then they just couldn't keep up. Seems like once they got to the home, they didn't last long. Just went. Their momma, my grandmother, lived to be 98. She dipped snuff and chased hogs outta the yard with a stick. I loved those women.

CV

True Friends

My grandfather said, "If you have as many true friends as fingers on one hand, you are a very rich person." True friends transform our journey from a lonely one to a voyage rich with the rewards of experience shared by a treasured soul mate.

FRIENDS

While working on this block, dear friends will come to mind. Won't you take a minute to write just a little about each one? What have you learned from each friend? How has each shared your life? What do you cherish most about each person? Use these ideas to inspire the fabrics in your Friendship Star, then maybe send each one a beautiful geranium!

Friendship Star

10" finished

Several measurements in this block fall on $\frac{1}{16}$" marks. Most rotary rulers do not show this mark.

To compensate, cut a little beyond the given measurement when you see a + sign. When you see a - sign, cut a bit shy of the measurement.

CUTTING RECIPE

A $2\frac{7}{8}$" → Cut 1 accent

B $2\frac{1}{2}$"+ → Cut 2 medium

C $4\frac{5}{8}$" → Cut 1 Background 1

D $3\frac{1}{4}$" → Cut 2 medium bright
2 medium dull
2 dark

E $3\frac{7}{8}$" → Cut 4 Background 1

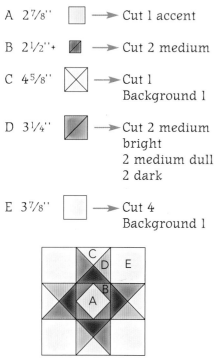

Step 1: Assemble the center.
Remember to use your matching marks when lining up triangles B with center A.

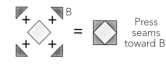

Press seams toward B.

Step 2: Make 4.

Step 3: Make 4.

Step 4: Make 4.

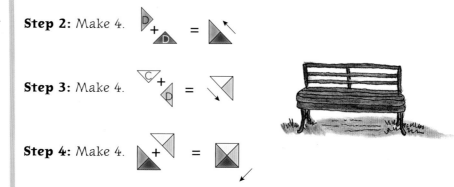

Once I lived in a place that had a beautiful playground between rows of apartments. A few kids played there but no adults were out and about. And when I went there, I had no place to sit and sew while I watched my kids. This place needed benches! We asked, and benches we got! After that, the playground was full of kids and grown-ups came out to sit and talk. Friendships and benches. Easy.

DCF

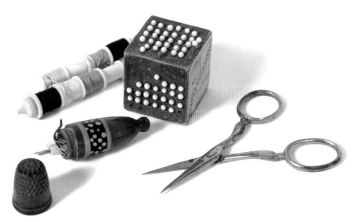

Step 5: Assemble the rows.

Rows 1 and 3

Row 2

Press open.

Step 6: Join rows together. Be extra careful to lock up intersections nicely.

Step 7: Make a tracing paper overlay for the lovely geranium. Appliqué to each E square. Now your Friendship Star shines as beautifully as all your friends.

Greater love has no one than this, that he lay

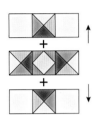

down his life for his friends. John 15:13

APPLIQUÉ PATTERN FOR GERANIUM

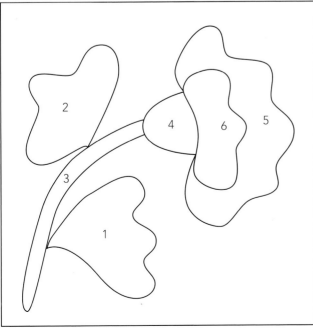

Believe nothing you hear,

half of what you see, and

only one-fourth of what

you know to be true.

A merry companion is music on a journey.

Traveling Sewing Kit
A Three-Piece Sewing Ensemble

Modern quilters often must sew on the go. I don't know about you, but my quilt projects are the first thing to go in the car as I head out for the day. Travel is made so much more attractive and efficient with this handsome sewing kit. A collapsible portfolio with a handsome monogram holds your quilt blocks safe and flat. Scissors, thread, a seam ripper, and even a cell phone fit comfortably in a small sewing bag. A tiny case provides a home for your treasured thimble, and a saucy strawberry pincushion completes the ensemble. We'll make the portfolio first. Ready, set, let's go!

WHAT YOU'LL NEED

- ½ yard decorator-weight fabric for portfolio cover with some left over for small bags
- ½ yard decorator-weight fabric for lining of portfolio with some left over for small bags
- 1 yard fleece for portfolio interlining and inner pages
- Fat quarter cream linen for basket background with some left over for small bags
- Fat quarter coordinating decorator-weight fabric for portfolio pocket
- ⅓ yard lace for pocket trim
- Large scraps for pieced basket and strawberry appliqué on portfolio front
- ½ yard fusible web. Please read and follow manufacturer's directions carefully.
- 45" tiny rickrack to edge basket block
- 1 yard ribbon or twine for closures
- Assorted buttons
- Embroidery floss and needle for monogram and strawberry embroidery
- 3" square of red or pink felt or wool for strawberry pincushion and a tiny bit of fiber fill stuffing
- 2" square of green felt or wool for strawberry top

Portfolio

15" x 15" finished

CUTTING RECIPE

15¹/₂" x 30¹/₂"
Cut 1 from portfolio cover fabric, and 1 from portfolio lining fabric.

18" x 34"
Cut 1 portfolio interlining from fleece.

14" x 28"
Cut 1 piece of fleece for portfolio pages.

14¹/₂" x 12¹/₂"
Cut 1 from pocket fabrics, which includes pocket self-lining.

10¹/₂" square
Cut 1 from linen for basket background.

The cutting recipe for the pieced basket on the portfolio cover is designed for fusing the pieces to the basket background. Therefore, the measurements do not include the seam allowance. Feel free to substitute another block of your choice for the strawberry basket. This is your portfolio and you can be as creative as you like in altering any part of it. Have fun!

Please note: It works best to fuse a large square of fusible web onto the wrong side of each fabric scrap before you cut out the individual triangles.

A   2"   →   Cut 1 light
                1 medium
                1 medium dark
                1 dark
                1 basket fabric

B   6"   →   Cut 1 basket fabric

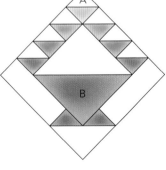

DECORATING THE PORTFOLIO COVER

Step 1: Construct the basket.
Arrange the A and B triangles on the 10¹/₂" square basket background following the diagram above. This is piecing without really piecing. When you are happy with the way it looks, fuse in place.

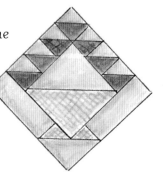

Step 2: Stitch a lovely monogram in the empty basket space. Use 3 strands of embroidery floss and a stem stitch.

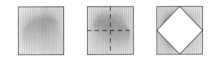

Step 3: Fuse basket to portfolio cover.
Apply fusible web to the backside of basket background. Center on portfolio cover. To find the center, fold cover in half as it will be when completed. Now crease this "book" in half and in quarters. Place the basket background on point over these centering creases. When you are satisfied with its position, fuse in place.

If you have one foot in yesterday and the other foot in tomorrow you're casting a shadow on today.

Step 4: To secure raw edges and to add decorative detailing, topstitch A and B triangles of the basket.

Step 5: Add strawberry appliqué. Use the appliqué design from page 46.
Trace each strawberry part onto the paper side of fusible web. Fuse to the appropriate red, green, and dark green fabric. Cut out on the traced line. Now position on your basket body. Fuse. Topstitch to secure raw edges.

Step 6: Add rickrack. Carefully stitch the tiny rickrack around the outer edge of the basket background. This secures the raw edges and adds a nice frame to the block.

He said one day out of the blue, "I'm leaving." Those words didn't hurt, they angered. I mean, wouldn't we all like to leave sometimes? Anyone can leave. That doesn't take anything except feet and a toothbrush. Staying is what's hard. That takes commitment.
DCF

INSIDE PORTFOLIO POCKET

Feel free to change the size of this pocket or to add one to the back of your portfolio as well.

Step 1: Fold pocket piece right sides together. Stitch, leaving an opening for turning.

14½"   Fold   Leave open

Step 2: Clip corners, turn, and press. Slipstitch opening closed.

Step 3: Add any decorative lace trim or more rickrack to the top edge of pocket.

Step 4: Position pocket on the left-hand side of portfolio lining. Topstitch in place.

JOINING LINING, INTERLINING, AND COVER

Step 1: Place portfolio cover and lining right sides together. Place these on top of the fleece interlining. Some of the fleece will extend beyond the cover; that's OK, it will be trimmed later. Pin well all around this sandwich.

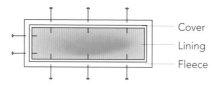

Cover
Lining
Fleece

Step 2: Place loop closures.
The portfolio closes with 3 buttons and loops, keeping your blocks clean and safe inside. Cut twine or ribbon into three 7" lengths. Tie each length into a loop using an overhand knot. Place loops between portfolio cover and lining on the right-hand side of sandwich as shown. Pin in place.

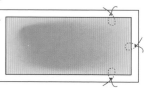

Step 3: Use a ¼" seam allowance to sew around portfolio, leaving an opening for turning. Clip corners, turn right side out, and carefully press. Slipstitch opening closed.

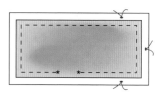

COMPLETING YOUR PORTFOLIO

Step 1: Position fleece "page" on top of the inside of the portfolio. Stitch down the center from top to bottom.

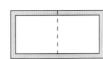

Step 2: Hand sew decorative buttons to the points of the basket background. These should coordinate with the loops to form perfect closures. The best part of this portfolio is its versatility! If need be, you can fold the portfolio in half and use the left button as a closure, making the portfolio even smaller. Brilliant!

Closed   or   closed even smaller

Sewing Bag
4'' x 7'' finished

Somewhere, anywhere, outta here!

CUTTING RECIPE

Use freezer paper to make templates A, B, and C.
A: Cut 1 from linen fabric for bag flap.
B: Cut 1 from leftover decorator-weight fabric for bag body.
C: Cut 1 from leftover decorator-weight fabric for lining.

Step 1: Assemble bag flap and body. Use a ¼'' seam to sew bag flap to body. Press seam toward flap.

Step 2: Trace strawberry design onto linen flap. Use your favorite embroidery stitches and 3 strands of floss to embroider the strawberries onto the bag flap.

Step 3: Place bag body/flap unit and lining right sides together. Stitch, leaving open between *'s. Clip corners, turn right side out, press, and slipstitch opening closed.

Step 4: Bring bottom edge of bag up to nearly meet flap. Hand whipstitch both sides closed in a neat seam. Now you should have a little sewing bag.

Step 5: Sew a button on the bag front. Attach a 12'' length of ribbon or twine to the flap with small hand stitches. Tie a bow around the button and you are ready for the road!

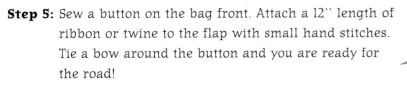

Thimble Holder
2'' x 3¾'' finished

Follow the steps for constructing the sewing bag, but use pattern pieces D, E, and F.
Sweet and oh so petite!

Strawberry Pincushion
1¾'' finished

Step 1: Use pattern piece G. Cut one from strawberry fabric. Place right sides together and stitch as indicated on pattern. Turn right side out.

Step 2: Use thread to match fabric and run a gathering stitch around the top of strawberry.

Step 3: Stuff berry with fiber fill. Pull gathering tight, knot and end off thread.

Step 4: Cut strawberry "top" from green felt or wool. Attach to strawberry with a length of embroidery floss, sewing the pincushion to your thimble bag at the same time. Darling!

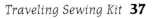

PATTERN FOR SEWING BAG

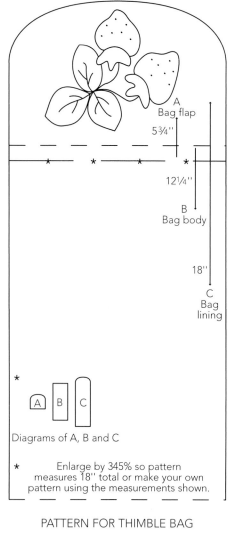

A
Bag flap

5¾"

★   ★   ★   ★   ★

12¼"

B
Bag body

18"

C
Bag lining

★

Ⓐ   B   C

Diagrams of A, B and C

★   Enlarge by 345% so pattern measures 18" total or make your own pattern using the measurements shown.

PATTERN FOR THIMBLE BAG

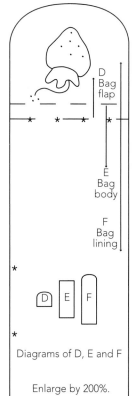

D
Bag flap

★   ★   ★   ★

E
Bag body

F
Bag lining

★

Ⓓ   E   F

Diagrams of D, E and F

Enlarge by 200%.

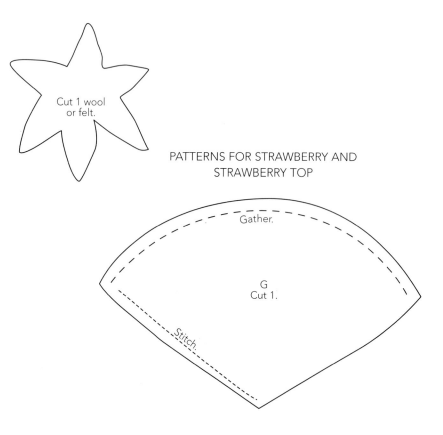

The dogs saw him first, curled up on the park bench. He had a black sleep mask over his eyes. (This fellow was used to the road and being out.) We were quiet, the dogs and I, as we got closer. The mask made him look like a pirate. He wore a bright T-shirt with a picture of a palm tree and an unreadable message on it. There was a tear on the shoulder and a bruised sore showed. His hair was light brown with soft curls. Tanned skin. A large duffel bag packed full was standing on the ground next to his head at the end of the bench. He never woke up as we passed him by.

It was early evening. Muggy but getting cooler and rain was supposed to come later that night. Where would he go and how? What did he need for the journey?

I came back later. Got a young teenager on a skateboard to come into the park with me. The fellow was still there. We left a bag for him. . .just a sandwich, something to wash up with, an apple, and a note. As we turned to go, I saw his method of travel—rollerblades! Well, roll on, son, and be safe. DCF

Cut 1 wool or felt.

PATTERNS FOR STRAWBERRY AND STRAWBERRY TOP

Gather.

G
Cut 1.

Stitch.

Churn Dash

Many hands make light work.

We are the lucky ones! We have found our passion in quilting. Blissfully we work with needle and thread, fabric and machine, pursuing the worthy art of making quilts. We start humbly as a beginning student, stumbling along with our first samplers. We take classes, read books, travel to symposiums, learn from friends, and make more quilts. We try the wide variety of quiltmaking techniques, searching for the ones we like best. With the persistence and diligence of the honeybee, we work to perfect our skills as we grow in our abilities. We are fine craftswomen in love with our craft.

Through our quilts, we express what's on our minds and in our hearts. This is our true work. It is scary revealing what is important to us. We need to take risks and stretch as we try to capture the vision that is the essence of our creative soul. We

How was I supposed to know these were beans? They looked like weeds to me.
Son to Mom

strive to honor our own distinctive tastes and styles, and focus inwardly for the inspiration to guide us. What we need to create our unique quilts is all right there inside of us. Looking closely and cherishing our individuality is much like the nectar of clover, the sweet reward of finding and doing our own meaningful work.

All work and no play make Jack a dull boy.

All work and no sewing and I'm feeling mad and sad. DCF

Work

A woman's work is never done. How true we know that to be! Dusting, dishes, laundry, cleaning, groceries, and cooking can seem like never-ending tasks. Although we don't have to make our own butter anymore, the Churn Dash block still resonates with modern-day symbolism of repetitive chores necessary to maintain a home. To combat this drudgery you can hire someone to get it done, bribe a child to help, or get the whole family involved to share in the labor. Anything to get us quickly to the work we truly love, our quilting.

TRAVEL LOG

One of the greatest lessons our journey offers is the discovery of our special gifts and talents. The pilgrimage to our most fulfilled self involves recognizing our abilities, cultivating them, and then sharing them with the world. Won't you take a moment to celebrate your gifts by listing them here? The world is made a more beautiful place by your generous sharing. Thank you for being you!

Churn Dash

10" finished

Have fun coloring this block to represent the work you love as well as the work you dislike.

CUTTING RECIPE

A 4⅞" Cut 2 Background
        2 dark

B 2½" Cut 4 Background
        4 medium
        1 dark

Step 1: Make 4.

Step 2: Make 4.

Step 3: Assemble the rows.

Rows 1 and 3

Row 2

Step 4: Join the rows, carefully matching intersections.

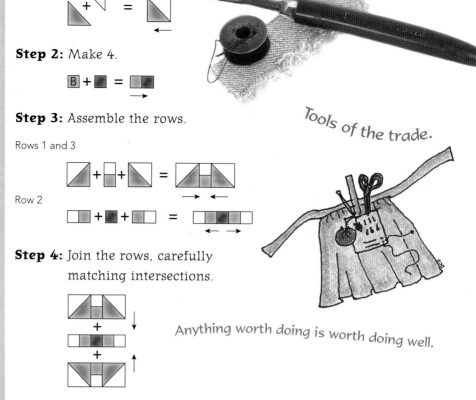

Tools of the trade.

Anything worth doing is worth doing well.

Step 5: Make a tracing paper overlay for the clover. Appliqué to background A's. Appliqué the bee onto center B. Embroider antennae with 2 strands of gold floss. Your beautiful work is now done!

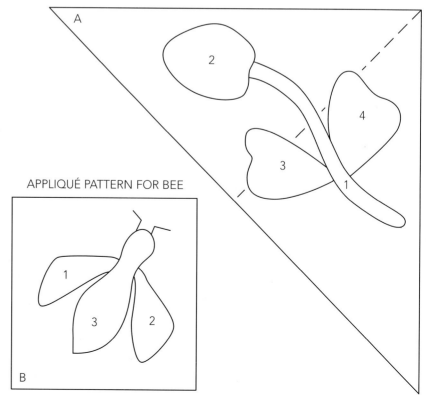

APPLIQUÉ PATTERN FOR CLOVER

APPLIQUÉ PATTERN FOR BEE

Tulip and Ivy

Layers of love unfold as we grow and mature into deep-hearted women. The giggles of a kindergarten love when we stubbornly insist on sharing the same seat with our beau give way to grade school puppy love, growing fuller with the breathlessness of our first real love. Texture and depth etch marks on our heart when it is broken by relationships that were not meant to be. We summon courage and faith to try again, hoping to find the kindred soul with whom we can share our lives. Wisdom gained through our direct experience blooms large as we finally find our one true love.

We discover, whether for a mate, a child, a parent, or a friend, love is like a delicate tulip. It must be tenderly nurtured in order to thrive. Attention, understanding, and acceptance are what dear hearts hunger for. The weeds of miscommunication, thoughtlessness, and neglect must be diligently and repeatedly pulled.

Trust and belief offer support when life's winds threaten. Forgiveness, as essential as water, ensures the flowering of love. It expands the heart, mends broken spirits on all sides, and refreshes with its cleansing.

As we gather knowledge of love along our way, we find our hearts grow ever larger. Our youthful, judgmental hearts soften with understanding and compassion. In full bloom we discover the treasure of not just loving, but persisting in love; love of our families, friends, and, most remarkably, love of ourselves.

Bloom where you are planted.

Love

The journey to love is perhaps the most confounding and challenging of all the roads we travel. Although we may share common depths and experiences of love, each of us is a pioneer in the unknown territory our hearts alone must take.

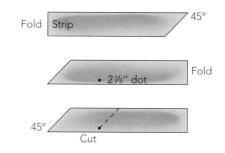

TRAVEL LOG

As a pioneer of the heart, what discoveries have you made about love that now guide and direct your way? What tendrils have you gathered that bind your love with the tenacity of the persistent ivy? Would you care to share what your heart knows here?

Tulip
10'' finished

Three concepts are introduced in this block. You'll learn how to cut parallelograms, how to accurately piece a Y-seam, and how to fold square D into a dimensional bud.

CUTTING RECIPE

A and AR (reverse):
   Cut one strip of medium fabric 1¼''+ x 45''.

Al and AlR (reverse):
   Cut one strip of medium-dark fabric 1½''+ x 45''.

B 4½''	⊠	Cut 2 Background 1
C 2''	□	Cut 4 Background 1
D 2½''		Cut 4 accent
E 3⅞''	◿	Cut 2 dark
F 1½''x 5''	▭	Cut 4 light or Background 1
G 1½''		Cut 1 medium dark

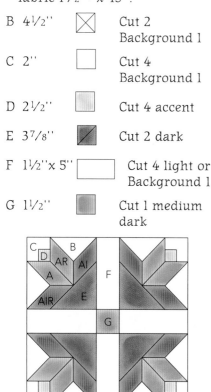

To cut A and AR, fold the strip of fabric in half. At the raw edge end, cut a 45° angle using the 45° mark on your ruler as a guide.

Turn your mat. Measure across the bottom of the strip 2⅞'' and use a pencil to mark a dot. Place the 45° line on your ruler along the bottom edge of the strip with the right edge of the ruler touching the pencil mark. Cut.

Continue marking and cutting to yield 4 pairs of A and AR. Keep these pairs together for ease in sewing later.

Fold | Strip | 45°

• 2⅞'' dot | Fold

45° | Cut

Repeat above instructions to cut Al and AlR from the medium-dark fabric. You now know how to cut parallelograms!

Step 1: When you begin sewing the Tulip block, pieces B, A, and AlR form a Y-seam. On the wrong side of each B, mark a dot ¼'' in from the right angle as shown.

B

Step 2: Stitch, following the number sequence in the diagram. Stop exactly at the dot and backstitch. Make 4.

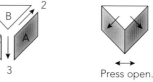

1   B   2
A1R   A
3

Press open.

Don't cut down the tree that gives you shade.

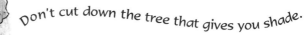

Step 3: Follow the above steps using pieces B, AR and AI. Make 4.

Press open.

Row 2

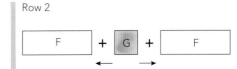

Step 9: Join the rows.

Step 4: Fold piece D into quarters and press.

D   ½   ¼

Step 5: Mark a dot on the wrong side of all C's, ¼'' in from the edge in one corner.

C.

Step 6: Place the folded D on the right side of C, matching raw edges in the corner with the pencil dot. Pin.

C • D

Step 7: Make 4.

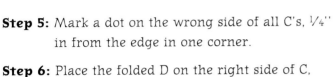

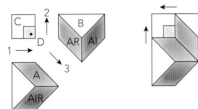

Step 8: Assemble the rows.

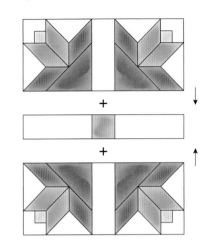

Step 10: Make a tracing paper overlay for ivy. Appliqué over the center portion of the block. Isn't your Tulip lovely?

Rows 1 and 3

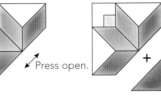

APPLIQUÉ PATTERN FOR IVY

The basis of world peace is the teaching which runs through almost all the great religions of the world' "Love thy neighbor as thyself.". . .

Eleanor Roosevelt

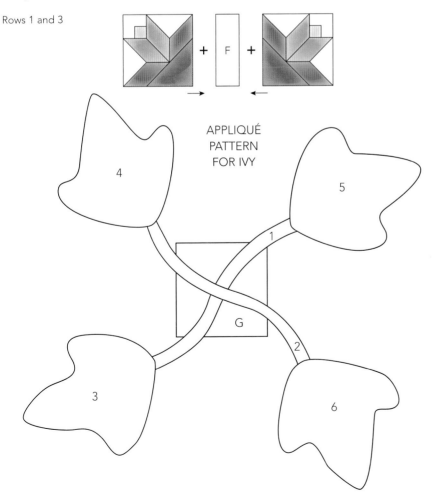

Strawberry Basket

This is not to say the relationship with our mothers is perfect. Is there a more complex relationship than that of mother and daughter? We are so much alike. This alone may be the source of the itching and irritation between us. Mother sees herself in her daughter. Daughter sees her reflection in her mother. It gets messy and muddy and sometimes downright explosive. But isn't that what widens and deepens a heart? Accepting each other in spite of our disagreements can be a defining moment in our voyage. Like the basket in our block, symbolizing maternal protection,

..........GENERATION GAPS..........

perhaps we can hold the beautiful, easy times right there next to the rocky, difficult ones. The simple act of holding and accepting is the beginning of unconditional love, a most potent lesson along our path to a beautifully expanded self.

Motherhood

Mother: The word conjures up so many memories, so many feelings. Our first startled exposure to the world is the calming protection of our mother's nurturing arms. She bathes, comforts, delights, and encourages us. She is the first to decipher our language, to answer our needs, to understand our spirit. She guides us little by little through the precarious steps of childhood, into the sunny days of elementary school, through the stormy confusion of our teen years, and finally into the wonder and responsibility of our adulthood. Then she performs the hardest feat of all: She lets us go. Standing aside, she watches as we struggle to find our wings, our courage, and our way, taking flight on our own precious journey.

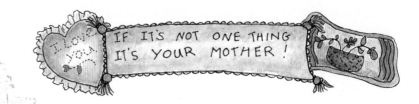

I LOVE YOU
IF IT'S NOT ONE THING IT'S YOUR MOTHER!

Prepare your children for the road, not the road for your children.

Strawberry Basket

10'' finished

Baskets are pieced just a bit differently than blocks put together in rows. Follow along to see how easy this goes together.

CUTTING RECIPE

A   2⅞''   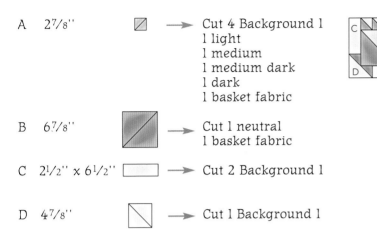 → Cut 4 Background 1
                       1 light
                       1 medium
                       1 medium dark
                       1 dark
                       1 basket fabric

B   6⅞''   → Cut 1 neutral
                       1 basket fabric

C   2½'' x 6½'' → Cut 2 Background 1

D   4⅞''   → Cut 1 Background 1

Step 1: Repeat with each color A to make 7 units.

Step 2:   **Step 3:**

Step 4:   **Step 5:**

Step 6:

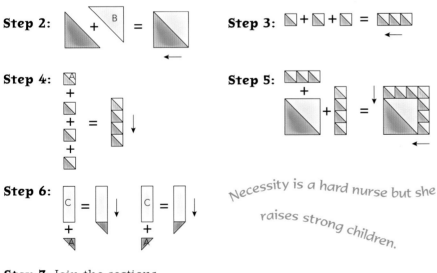

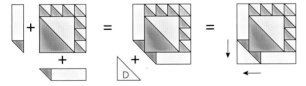

Necessity is a hard nurse but she raises strong children.

Step 7: Join the sections.

Step 8: Make a tracing paper overlay for the strawberries. Match the horizontal guideline to the top edge of basket fabric B. Center the vertical guideline with the basket center. Delicious!

TRAVEL LOG

Thoughts of my mother "colored" this block from its inception. She was a stunning redhead with a fiery temperament. When I think of her, I think warm, colorful, creative. She was a talented seamstress, clothing her five children elegantly. She loved to garden, turning an acre of Colorado wilderness into an impressive oasis. More than anything, she was creative to the bone.

Now I am blessed with a most extraordinary daughter of my own. Thoughts of her also colored my basket, for she is a beautiful strawberry blonde with so many of the attributes of her grandmother. Together we continue the learning begun with my mother, holding and accepting the delights of our relationship alongside its irritations. What thoughts will color your basket?

My mother used to fill a bathtub up so high with water, put our dirty clothes in, then some detergent, and just let the little kids jump around on the clothes. That's how we washed clothes.

ES

I want to share a very special recipe with you that is a family favorite from my mother, Helen Christensen. She loved her kitchen, baking the world's most incredible cinnamon rolls and stirring up batches of gourmet toffee each and every Christmas. This recipe for her famous Pineapple Carrot Loaf is easy and extra yummy. Try serving it at your next quilting bee.

When I was coming up we didn't have nothing. Once I remember Mama wantin' to go out ta eat. But we didn't have no money back then. Well, we heard about a wreck happening up the road and went out to see it. Then Mama saw some folks she knowed up the bend. So up we went. And, right there in that bend Mama found a twenty-dollar bill.
"Let's go eat!" says Mama.
South Carolina store conversation

PINEAPPLE CARROT LOAF

Makes 3 small loaves

1. Preheat oven to 350°. Grease and flour 3 small loaf pans.

2. Mix together:
   - 3 cups sifted flour
   - 2 cups sugar
   - 1 tsp. baking soda
   - 1 tsp. salt
   - 1 tsp. cinnamon
   - 1½ cups oil
   - 3 eggs
   - 2 tsp. vanilla
   - small can crushed pineapple; reserve 7 tsp. liquid for glaze
   - 1½ cups chopped pecans or walnuts
   - 2 cups grated carrots

3. When all of the above ingredients are mixed thoroughly, pour into the loaf pans.

4. Bake for about one hour. Cool slightly, then glaze with the following thin but delicious glaze.

GLAZE
   - 7 tsp. reserved pineapple juice
   - 1 cup powdered sugar

Mix until smooth. Enjoy!

APPLIQUÉ PATTERN FOR STRAWBERRIES

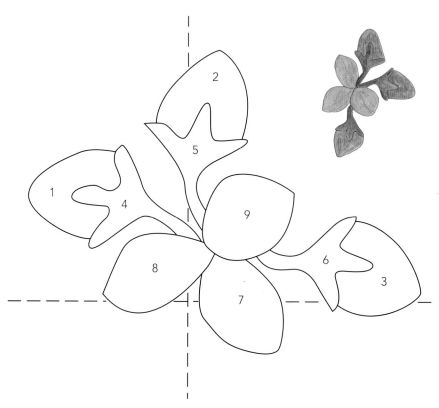

Hearth and Home

It's spring and I'm furiously working in my garden. New shoots of green surprise me everywhere. The air is just the right temperature for serious digging and I find myself lost in thoughts of garden plans. Something catches my eye. There, high in the enormous oak tree that shades my backyard, I spot a blue jay. She is coming in for a landing with a parcel of twigs clutched tightly in her beak. I watch for a minute and quickly understand she is building a nest. Oh joy!

For the next three days, the jay and I work relentlessly side by side. She is building her sturdy nest in the precarious limbs of the oak; I am on my hands and knees digging in the dirt. Both of us are "feathering our nests," improving the condition of our homes. I marvel at her innate sense of architecture. She seems to know exactly what she is doing. Trip after tiresome trip, she arrives with just the right material to ensure a safe birthing place for her new babies. As she makes each new addition, I notice her sitting down in the nest as if she's trying it on for size. She works and wrestles the tiny twigs until all is to her liking. She seems to know instinctively what a perfect home should feel like.

Most of us create many a home in the course of our life's journey. Our humble first abode with its hand-me-down furniture is one we will always (fondly?) remember.

Safe Haven

Some of us live in different homes as life changes. With each new address, we gain a better vision of just what it takes to create a refuge for ourselves. After many tries, like the diligent blue jay, we begin to confidently trust our instincts for finding the critical building blocks for our home. Skillfully we apply the mortar of understanding, trust, and forgiveness to the bricks of love; these components are much more important than the color of the couch. At last, as the stewards of the hearth where so much learning and growing occur, we trust our ability to create the nurturing, welcoming place we call home.

Home is where the heart is, and the unwashed, the unfed, and the unmade.

TRAVEL LOG

This is a lovely opportunity to reflect on the homes you've lived in. Is there a favorite that comes to mind? What are the unique qualities vital to the atmosphere of your home? I found a fabric printed with acorns and oak leaves to use in my block, symbolizing the strength and solidity necessary for a sound foundation to my home.

Feel free to change the number of eggs in your nest to reflect the members of your family, and I'll keep you posted on how many babies the blue jay has.

Hearth and Home

10" finished

This is a simple block made beautiful by dramatic colors.

CUTTING RECIPE

A   2½" x 6½"
⟶ Cut 1 medium light

B   2½"
⟶ Cut 2 medium light
4 dark
4 medium
4 Background 1

C   2⅞"
⟶ Cut 4 dark
4 Background 1

You know it's hard to leave your house for the nursing home. You young folks can't imagine. I hated giving up the old bed I slept in all the years with my husband. I had lost my husband and now the bed.
Mrs. W

Step 1: Make 8.

◣ + ◥ = ◪
←

Step 2: Assemble the rows.

Rows 1 and 5

B + ◣ + B + ◪ + B = [◣ B ◪ B]

Rows 2 and 4

◥ + ▦ + ☐ + ▦ + ◢ = [◥ ▦ ☐ ▦ ◢]

Row 3

▦ + A + ▦ = [▦ A ▦]

Step 3: Join the rows.

Press open.

Press open.

Step 4: Make a tracing paper overlay for the sweet nest. Stitch in the center of your cozy Home block and stand back to admire your great work!

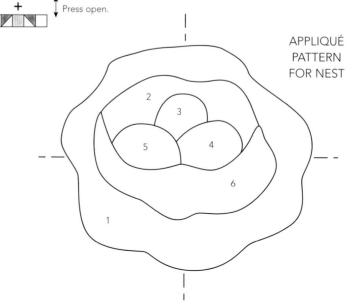

APPLIQUÉ
PATTERN
FOR NEST

SWISS CHEESE ONION PIE

- ◆ 1 cup saltine cracker crumbs
- ◆ ¼ cup melted butter

Mix crumbs with melted butter and press into 9" pie plate.
Set aside.

- ◆ 3 cups thinly sliced onions
- ◆ ¼ cup butter
- ◆ ½ lb. grated swiss cheese
- ◆ 1 cup scalded milk
- ◆ 1 Tbsp. flour
- ◆ 1 tsp. salt
- ◆ 3 well beaten eggs

Cook onions in ¼ cup of butter till tender but not brown,
place in crumb crust. Combine cheese with flour and salt,
add eggs and milk. Pour over the onions. Bake in slow
oven at 350° for 40 minutes. Serves 6 to 8.

When I had to leave my old house, which was
much bigger, for this small one, it was hard.
I had so much stuff. So, I made two rules for
myself about what I would take:
I had to need it, and I had to love it.

DCF

If a house is divided against
itself, that house cannot stand.

Mark 3:25

Good fences make good neighbors.

EVERYTHING IS SOMEwhere!

"Normal" is only a cycle
on a washing machine.

We shall not cease from exploration
And the end of all our exploring
Will be to arrive where we started
And know the place for
the first time. . .

T.S. Eliot

Chirp!

Rambler

If anything is constant in this life it is change. Rarely do we grow up to live in the hometown of our birth. Even if we do, it's likely for dear friends and family members to move away, taking a part of our hearts with them. In this day and age, change seems to happen at the speed of light. Companies change hands, relocate, downsize, or merge, leaving personal lives in a tailspin. How, oh how, are we to cope?

The Rambler block is a fitting pattern, symbolizing change at many levels. It looks as if it's headed in all directions at once, much like our complex modern lives. Yet if we look closely, we see a soft safe center, pointing the way to our "true north." If we can somehow find the time to stop, to breathe, to look at this very moment, we find the calm and peaceful grounding of the present. Everything is easier, lighter, more understandable if we can simply slow down to enjoy the treasures found in "now." The tiny bloom of the forget-me-not calls a reminder to our harried souls. Stop worrying about all the change, it will happen anyway. If we can leverage the time to savor the quiet of just this moment we are rewarded with a startling surprise—growth!

Change

I grew up a nomad. Half the year my family lived on the edge of the Colorado desert. There our thousands of sheep could graze through the light snows of winter and safely birth their lambs in the gentle spring. Then a huge migration took us to the cool alpine mountains near Aspen where the lush summer meadows fatten the herd. I was never quite ready for these twice-yearly moves. Even though part of me dreaded them, they always offered freshness. New friends, new scenery, new adventures gave my youth increased experience and character.

Well, just tell me how to get from here to there or are we lost yet?

TRAVEL LOG

Change happens on many levels. There are the many moves that so upend us. There is the transplanting of others, which leaves us behind, hollow and sad. For many there is the inevitable empty nest when children finally find their wings and fly. And there is change on a deeply personal level as we discover the need to listen to our heart. The journey of inner transformation compels us to uncover our focus, our resilience, our passion, and our love. What change comes to mind as you consider this design? How can you represent this growth as you shade your Rambler block?

Rambler

The only person you can change is yourself.

10" finished

The main part of this block is made with Flying Geese units. For a quick review of this easy piecing technique, see page 23.

CUTTING RECIPE

A	2¼" x 4"		→	Cut 4 dark 4 medium
B	2¼"		→	Cut 16 light
C	3⅜"		→	Cut 2 medium light
D	4"		→	Cut 1 accent
E	6¼"		→	Cut 1 Background 1

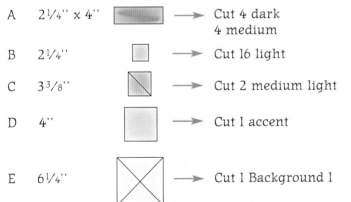

Step 1: Make 4 Flying Geese units using the dark A and light B. Make 4 units using the medium A and light B.

Step 2: Make 4.

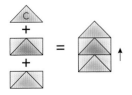

You know, you can stay stuck in one place never dreaming of the good things up ahead, around the bend, outta sight.
Reflection

Step 3: Assemble the diagonal rows.

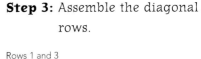

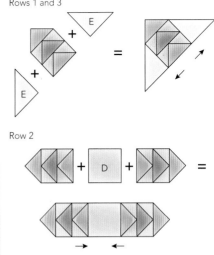

Step 4: Join the rows, carefully matching intersections.

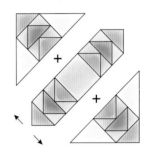

Step 5: Make a tracing paper overlay for the forget-me-not. Appliqué to D. Perfect!

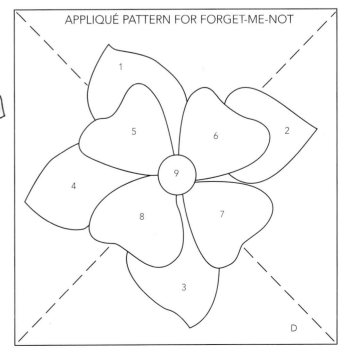

APPLIQUÉ PATTERN FOR FORGET-ME-NOT

Broken Star

Some bumps are mere disappointments. Plans don't work out, relationships change or fade, quilt designs end up in shreds on the workroom floor. These are discouraging, but often with a closer look, we see things have turned out for the better because of the rough spot. We get a clearer picture of where we are going, a sharper focus on our direction, and more insight into who we are.

CAUTION FALLING ROCK!

Other bumps feel like we've driven off a cliff, only to miserably hang by the weakest of threads. How quickly the road can change! One minute all is well as we cruise down the highway of our lives. Then in an instant, everything changes. With a simple phone call, our world is shattered in a million pieces with loss so overwhelming we can hardly breathe. Our path narrows to a faint whisper.

How do we go on? How do we put back together the broken pieces of our world? The process is much like piecing this Broken Star. We start. With a trembling faith, we pick up our needle and ply it with a tiny strand of hope. We work slowly. Tenderly, gingerly we stitch one piece to another. We marvel that anything can possibly emerge from this overwhelming grief, but it does. We see the beauty and the strength, this glowing seam of our soul.

Loss

There are bound to be bumps along any road. Among the countless miles of every path, there are certain to be challenges in the terrain. Sharp curves slow us down, wrong turns leave us feeling lost, steep inclines test our stamina, U-turns redirect us, and jarring bumps stun us with their force. So it is with the journey of our lives.

WORRIES   CARES   WOES

"PACK UP All YOUR CARES AND ......"

TRAVEL LOG

For hundreds of years, the weeping willow has been a symbol of loss and grief. We join legions of women who have gone before us, pointing the way to cope with such disappointments. As you stitch this block, consider the stamina and wisdom gained from the bumps your journey has offered you.

Broken Star

10'' finished

Use the Flying Geese method of assembly for piecing D and E. Sharp points are the reward for carefully sewing this handsome star.

CUTTING RECIPE

A   3''   □ → Cut 4 Background 1
                 1 medium

B   2⁵/₈''   ◹ → Cut 4 medium dark
                 2 light

C   6¼''   ⊠ → Cut 1 Background 1

D   2¼'' x 4'' ▭ → Cut 4 medium

E   2¼''   ▪ → Cut 8 dark

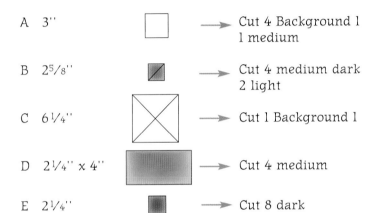

Step 1: Make 4.

Step 2: Assemble the center.

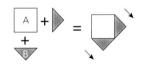

Press toward B's.

Step 3: Make 4 Flying Geese units using D and E.

When my dog Lucy died,
I mourned for weeks.
Sounds dumb, I know, but
every day she was so
excited to see me.
She just twirled around
with joy. On cold fall days,
she tore around
the yard going faster
and faster. She could
smile too. Really.

DCF

I remember the day I went
up to my room seeking
comfort from a pile of
comic books and a doll to
hold. The comics and doll
were of no interest to me
that day or ever again. I
had outgrown them.

Childhood memory

Step 4: Make 4.

Step 5: Assemble the rows.

Rows 1 and 3

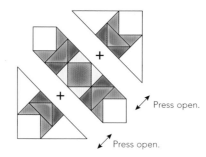

Row 2

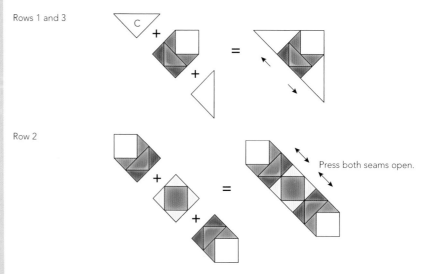

Press both seams open.

Step 6: Join rows together along the diagonal.

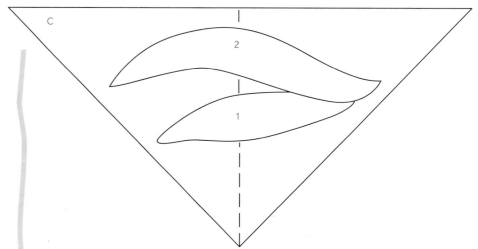

Press open.

Press open.

Step 7: Make a tracing paper overlay for the willow sprigs.
Appliqué to each C.

APPLIQUÉ PATTERN FOR WILLOW SPRIGS

C

2

1

Passionate Star

Our passions are a direct link to our hearts. The things we love give us clues to the deepest connections with our creative spirits. The gardens we tend with such devotion offer design ideas for countless quilts. The books we savor over and over again provide themes around which we build our next creation. Our pets gift us with their humor, adding spunky uniqueness to our quilts. When we feel passionate about something, our hearts race, we go weak in the knees, we become obsessed, everything seems lighter, we are filled with joy. Herein lies the secret passage to our best work.

Focusing on what we truly love helps guide us through the maze of innumerable quiltmaking techniques and styles. We set the true course of our own quilt path as we gradually begin to narrow our choices. The best way to guarantee sure footing is to follow as closely as possible the delights of our hearts. Looking at what we love, honoring it by utilizing it in our work, allowing our passions to sweep us to new horizons—all guide us to a style uniquely our own. Our work develops a personal imprint, our hallmark. Our steady compass is the ever-changing but always-satisfying passions that define who we are.

To thine own self be true.

Oh, golly gee. I just love little delicate pinks and sweet soft greens and best of all piecing. Ooooooooo, I do!

Cool sister! I really dig mod designs and appliqué is right with me. Give me those jazzy stripes in bold colors and man, I'm on fire!

Joy

Look into the eyes of a quilter as she tells you the many reasons she loves anything green and you'll see unabashed passion. Her voice becomes animated. Her hands begin to fly, and her eyes light up. Her entire face beams with an inner glow. She is head-over-heels in love with her world of green!

TRAVEL LOG

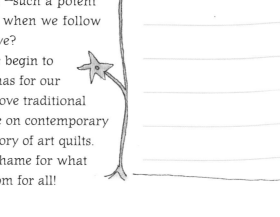

The points of this star symbolize the many aspects of our passion. They lead us in the direction of our most authentic work. The center sunflower means "turn to the sun"—such a potent reminder that we shine brightest when we follow our hearts. What is it that you love?

May we as quilters everywhere begin to appreciate the passion each of us has for our craft, celebrating with those who love traditional quilts, supporting those who thrive on contemporary work, and admiring the new territory of art quilts. May we never make another feel shame for what she loves, but generously make room for all!

Groan, Growing, Growth.

Don't give in or up now!

When you see a - (minus), simply align your ruler a little less than the given measurement. When you see a + (plus), align it a bit beyond the given measurement.

Passionate Star

10'' finished

You'll love these tips for cutting and accurately stitching isosceles triangles. Some of the measurements fall in between the $1/8$'' marks on the ruler.

CUTTING RECIPE

A $4^5/8$''- x $2^3/8$''   ▷ ⟶ Cut 4 medium dark

To cut A's, first cut a strip of fabric $2^3/8$'' x 22''. Fold in half with wrong sides together. Cut 2 rectangles $2^3/8$'' x $4^5/8$''-. Now cut on the diagonal. Keep A and AR's together as pairs.

B $4^1/4$'' -   ▽ ⟶ Cut 4 Background 1

To cut B's, cut a strip of fabric $4^1/4$''- x 18''. Mark a dot every $4^1/4$''- along the top edge. Fold to find the halfway point between the dots. Mark that point on the bottom edge. Now mark every $4^1/4$''- along this new edge. Connect the dots with your ruler as shown and cut.

$4^1/4$ -

Joy is not in things. It's in us.

C   2⅛''   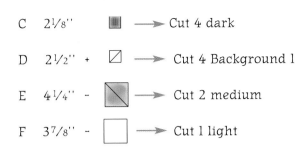 → Cut 4 dark

D   2½'' + → Cut 4 Background 1

E   4¼'' - → Cut 2 medium

F   3⅞'' - → Cut 1 light

Step 1: Lining up pieces A and B can be a little confusing. With a pencil, draw in the ¼'' seam allowance on all points on A's, AR's, and all B's. This gives you an X to help you accurately match each point.

A   B   AR

Step 2: Make 4.

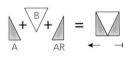
A   AR   ←   →

Step 3: Make 4.

D
+
D + C   =   ↑
←

APPLIQUÉ PATTERN FOR SUNFLOWER

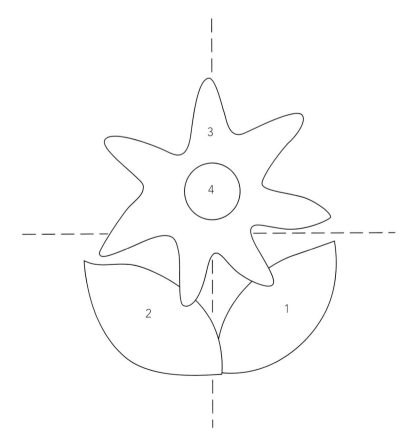

You know what I just love? Surprises! Sometimes it's in the making of a quilt. All of a sudden, there it is; colors that just bounce and blend and present themselves as pure joy! And other times it's in my yard, which is quite wild, actually—the gift of an unplanted flower blooming away in the first morning light. "Well, hey there!" I say to it. "Where did you come from?" Or, maybe this is the best: after a soft summer rain, baby box turtles hatching out, no bigger than quarters. Every day is just a gift, and, most of the time, I'm so thankful.

DCF

Step 4: Make 4.

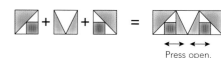

Step 5: Assemble the rows.

Rows 1 and 3

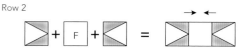

Press open.

Row 2

Joy to the world.

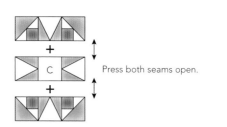

Step 6: Join the rows.

Press both seams open.

Step 7: Make a tracing paper overlay for the sunflower. Stitch to center of F. Bravo!

Smile and the world smiles with you. . .

MEGAN'S FAVORITE SINFUL CHOCOLATE TORTE

You will need one pound cake from the freezer section of your grocery store. Thaw slightly as you make the following frosting.

- 6-ounce package semi-sweet chocolate chips
- ¼ cup butter
- 1 tsp. vanilla
- 4 egg yolks
- 2 Tbsp. confectioners' sugar

Watch this closely, melting everything together and stirring constantly. When mixture begins to thicken, whisk vigorously with a whisk or hand beater until shiny, dark, and thick.

Remove from heat. Cool slightly.

Slice thawing pound cake into as many layers as you can. I usually manage about four. Place the bottom layer on a serving dish and coat with chocolate. Top with a cake slice, frost again, and continue until you have put your cake back together. Frost the top, sides, and end of cake.

Diamond Star

As we proceed, we learn the wisdom of traveling light. Through meaningful experience, we come to understand less really is more. Now we know what we need, and often it is the simplest of things. With more certainty, we carve out time and space for our quilting. With tenacity, we guard these from intrusions. We let go of unwanted obligations like a clean house or always being the one to volunteer. We engineer a calmer, simpler environment where each object is genuinely appreciated, each activity enthusiastically embraced. Like this Diamond Star, our choices shine with elegant simplicity.

As we rest a little longer, we may take note of how strong we've grown. Through determined work, we've come to know our own minds and to finally summon the will to voice them. Liberated from worries of what others might think, we joyously move now to our own drumbeat. Our pilgrimage has taught us patience, persistence, acceptance, and faith—just a few of the many facets of our precious diamond soul.

*Come unto me all you who
are weary and burdened
and I will give you rest.*
Matthew 11:28

Strength

Are you weary, dear quilter? Let's rest for a moment and reflect together on the many miles we've come. It feels sweet to look across the distance and see how much we've learned, how deeply we've grown. The way has not always been easy, but as rough spots appeared, we've repeatedly seen how capably we cope with our lives. This is not to say we do things perfectly. We have ferocious outbursts and dark periods of doubt. But when all is said and done, somehow we do manage. We make slow but sure progress along this path to our fullest, most incredible selves. This is definitely worth noting.

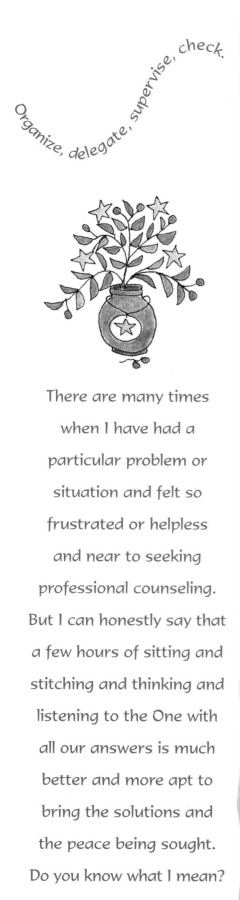

Organize, delegate, supervise, check.

There are many times when I have had a particular problem or situation and felt so frustrated or helpless and near to seeking professional counseling. But I can honestly say that a few hours of sitting and stitching and thinking and listening to the One with all our answers is much better and more apt to bring the solutions and the peace being sought. Do you know what I mean?

Email exchange

TRAVEL LOG

So here we are, resting on our "laurels." Doesn't it feel grand? Laurel means perseverance and glory, just the ingredients necessary for our expedition. Would you care to note what triumphs you've had lately? What have you been able to let go of to simplify and enhance your life? Just as students of old would wear a laurel wreath to celebrate their accomplishments, so we, too, can enjoy our victories with this block!

Diamond Star

10'' finished

Once again we'll use Y-seam construction to form this star. Be patient and precise!

CUTTING RECIPE

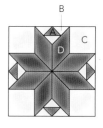

A	$2^3/8$''	◩	→	Cut 2 dark 2 Background 1
B	$3^1/4$''+	⊠	→	Cut 2 Background 1
C	$3^1/2$''	☐	→	Cut 4 Background 1
D	$2^1/2$''+ x 22''	◢	→	Cut 4 dark 4 medium dark

To cut diamonds, first cut a strip of each fabric $2^1/2$''+ x 22''. Cut one end of strip at a 45° angle. Turn your cutting mat. Line up the $2^1/2$''+ mark on your ruler with this 45° cut edge. The 45° mark of your ruler should be parallel with the bottom of your strip. Cut. Move your ruler over $2^1/2$''+ until you've cut 4 diamonds from each strip.

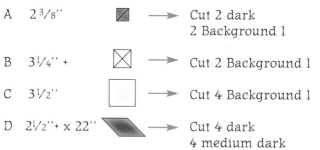

Step 1: Make 4.

Step 2: Make 4.

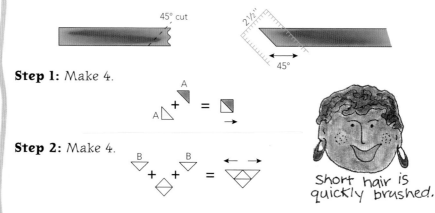

short hair is quickly brushed.

Step 3: Mark a dot ¼″ on seam allowance A/B units and all C's.

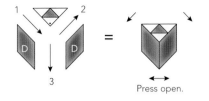

Step 4: Use Y-seam construction; stop at the dots to make 4.

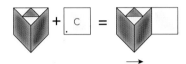

Press open.

Step 5: Add a C square to each of the A/B/D units.

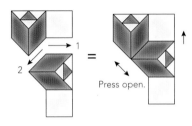

Step 6: Join 2 of the A/B/D/C units together. Repeat.

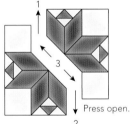

Press open.

Step 7: Join the 2 star halves, following the arrows and stopping at the dots. Easy does it!

Press open.

Step 8: Make a tracing paper overlay for the laurel leaves. Appliqué to each C. Your Diamond Star is stunning.

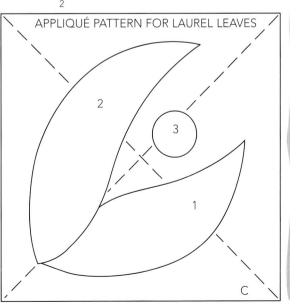

APPLIQUÉ PATTERN FOR LAUREL LEAVES

2

3

1

C

WOMEN ARE LIKE TEABAGS....THEY DON'T KNOW HOW STRONG THEY ARE UNTIL THEY GET IN HOT WATER.....
ELEANOR ROOSEVELT

On September 11th, 2001, I realized something important as the events unfolded. I heard about the first airplane while still at home, then the next two at an attorney's office, then the last after I arrived at my place of work. I thought, "This is the end." I told everyone they could leave and go home, and I thought I would, too. I wondered what I would do at home. Finish a quilt I was working on? No, that wouldn't do. That didn't matter anymore. Why finish? Well, then a new thought. I would garden. That would bring comfort. Nope. That wouldn't work; no sense in weeding on the "last day." No, if it was over, it was over. I'd just wait. I felt peaceful with that thought. My only regret? I wished I was leaving with nothing left, that I had given away more to help others.

DCF

Profound Pillow

11½" x 13½" finished
Designed by Diane Frankenberger

Sometimes we need a visual reminder of what's important in our lives. Here are the basic instructions for making a Profound Pillow, perfect for center stage on a couch, chair, or bed. Feel free to use any of the quotes or sayings found throughout the book to create your own "profound-ness."

WHAT YOU NEED

- One 8" x 10" muslin, linen, or osnaburg fabric piece for pillow top center
- One 12" x 14" light gray fabric to be used as pillow top liner
- One 12" x 14" fabric for pillow back
- One 12" x 14" fabric for pillow lining
- 4 fabric strips that coordinate with pillow embroidery; cut these 1¾" x 14"
- Embroidery floss for stitching words and stems
- Assorted buttons for flowers
- Large-eye needle
- 1 bag polyfil
- Water-erasable pen

After your fling watch for the sting.

Step 1: Trace the words, flowers, and stems onto the pillow top center; placing the pattern and fabric on a window or lightbox works well. Use a water-erasable pen or light pencil mark.

Step 2: Using 2 or 3 strands of embroidery floss, stitch sayings and stems. To make sure your knot stays on the wrong side of the fabric, place your needle in between the strands as shown. Use a running stitch or a back stitch.

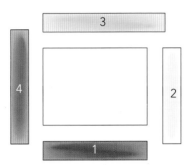

Step 3: Sew buttons on for flowers. Have great fun with this, creating new varieties to please yourself.

Step 4: Sew the 1³/₄" strips around pillow top center, placing right sides together. Use a ¹/₄" seam allowance. Press seams toward strip. Trim even with pillow top or with the last strip you sewed on.

Step 5: Baste the light gray liner behind the pillow top. Trim to fit.

Step 6: Layer your pillow parts: first the back lining, then the pillow back with the right side up, and finally the pillow top with the right side down. Pin. Stitch around all sides, leaving an opening for turning. Turn right side out. Stuff until plump. Slipstitch opening closed. Admire your pillow. . .and heed the words!

EMBROIDERY PATTERN FOR PROFOUND PILLOW
Enlarge by 200%.

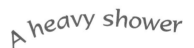

A heavy shower is soon over.

Harvest Bouquet

It is the dog days of summer. Heat has kept me inside for weeks now. A rare treat greets me this morning—cool fresh air has returned, however briefly. I eagerly launch my morning walk. In short order I pass not one but two elderly lady neighbors tackling their yards with lawn mowers. There they are, not a day less than seventy, their hips full and round, their bosoms heavy, their heads covered by sensible broad-brimmed hats. Their grit and spunk send me reeling. As I watch the smiles of greeting cross their faces, I am struck by how luscious, how wise, and how absolutely beautiful these dear older women are. I whisper a humble prayer. "Please, may I grow up to be just like them!"

Long miles from the innocence of our childhood through the steep inclines of love and work, we finally arrive at this delightful vantage point. We stop in the quiet of a breathtaking vista to survey, with a well-earned perspective, the road below. We gather together bits and pieces of our journey, symbols that have marked our way. It is a rich feeling to harvest acorns, the potential and dreams of our youth; buttercups to remind us of our grandmother's tender devotion; strawberries from our mother; geraniums blooming in friendship; forget-me-nots marking all the change we've seen; the sunflower pointing the way to our beloved passions; and the sweet clover and honey bee telling all how much we adore our work. Tied together, these experiences, these milestones, become a glorious bouquet of all the wisdom we have gathered.

Wisdom is listening and learning from those who have gone before us on life's journey.

Today is that TOMORROW you thought about yesterday.

TRAVEL LOG

Four lovely triangles of appliqué form a circle of stunning abundance. As we stitch each tiny piece, we begin to feel the peacefulness of our life journey. With each delicate stitch, we can measure and count the wisdom we have gained. The dictionary describes wisdom as understanding what is true, right, or lasting. It will be different for each of us, for we each walk a unique path. Won't you take a moment to note your thoughts about the wisdom you hold? Like the two marvelous wise women of my summer morning, each of us can inspire others with the wisdom we have earned.

Harvest Bouquet
14⅛'' finished corner triangles

It's time to stitch the delicious appliqué triangles; this is when our peace with time truly shines. Slow down and enjoy each stitch as you gather the bits of wisdom we've explored together.

CUTTING RECIPE

In order to avoid distorting the long bias edge of each of these triangles during the sewing process, a full square is used. This is very sturdy and allows us to stitch two appliqué triangles on one 18'' square. We will true these up once the entire appliqué is complete.

Cut two 18'' x 18'' squares of Background 2.

Step 1: Using an iron, crease each square on the diagonal from one corner to the opposite corner. Do this in just one direction. Baste with a contrasting thread along this crease mark. You now have a diagonal guideline.

Step 2: Baste the corner of each background triangle and a positioning guideline: On the wrong side of each background square, establish the corner intersected by your diagonal guideline. Use a 15'' square ruler to draw in the corner. Draw the line 14⅛'' long and at least 1'' inside the fabric edge as shown. Then use a ruler or yardstick to draw a diagonal line from marked corner to marked corner to use as a guide to center the appliqué design.

Wrong side

14⅛''

She speaks with
wisdom and
faithful instruction
is on her tongue.

Proverbs 31:26

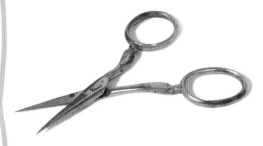

Experience is the best teacher.

HIGH IS THE ROOF BUT THE GATE IS LOW.

Use contrasting thread to baste along the drawn lines form-
ing the corner. Pivot the square and repeat on the opposite
corner for the second triangle.

Step 3: Make a tracing paper overlay for the appliqué. Feel free to
add or change any of the gathered flowers to reflect your
heart's desire. I changed the corner of one triangle to feature
the sweet nest from the Hearth and Home block. I simply
traced it on a small piece of tracing paper and taped it in
place on my overlay. No need to redraw the entire overlay.

Step 4: Stitch the appliqué.
Follow the numbered sequence to stitch each
appliqué in place. For a unified look, use the
same fabrics you used for the appliqué in the
pieced blocks. Line the corner marks and
diagonal line of your tracing paper overlay
over the corresponding basted lines on your background for
the correct placement of each piece. Savor the moment!

Step 5: True up the appliqué triangles. When complete, you will have
2 squares that each have 2 appliqué corners. Truing these up
into actual triangles is easy.
Work on the wrong side of each square.
Confirm once again the corner measures
14 ⅛". With a long ruler and a pencil,
connect the 2 right-angle sides to form the
hypotenuse side. This line should measure 20". You should see
a complete triangle before you. Make sure all the appliqué
falls within the triangle and seems centered.

Wrong side

20"

Once you are satisfied, use your ruler to add a ¼" seam
allowance and cut with a rotary cutter. DO NOT CUT ON THE
PENCIL LINE! There, you have your stunning Harvest Bouquet.

Add ¼" with
ruler and cut.

Bee's wings are cut and
appliquéd as one piece.

APPLIQUÉ PATTERN FOR
HARVEST BOUQUET

Enlarge by 200%.

14 1/8''

Blazing Star

The Blazing Star seems perfect for the center of our quilt. Look with me at all it symbolizes. Can you see the beauty, formed from deep within? We've learned to consult our inner compass for guidance as we create and as we live. More and more we focus within instead of searching for answers from without. The genius that is uniquely ours radiates outward in echoes of color, glowing more glorious with expanded beauty.

See the dark and light layers. The shadows of disappointments, challenges, and struggles add a precious depth and richness to this star, and to our lives. The peaks and valleys of our journey have taught us much, tempered us greatly, and given us the certain knowledge that we can persevere to the very end.

Round and round the Blazing Star spins, much like the cycles of our lives. We learn a lesson, make a discovery, experience change only to find we come full

circle once again. There are new journeys to begin, but this time we are a little wiser, more experienced, and perhaps a tiny bit braver. We eagerly embrace the chance for fresh vistas and the promise of untried roads. They lead us to further grow within this splendid thing we call our soul.

Can you sense the rhythm of the star? Like the perfect pace we find in our particular travel gait, we stitch this star together in our own good time. Slowing down to appreciate each stitch, each step along the way, we find the sweetest peace. Here in the harbor of our hearts, we are at peace with time, sharing with the world our best: a woman's journey stitched in cloth!

Destination

I think it's called an epiphany, and I'm sure I had one. I was on the road truly through the mountains one fall. The sky was a deep, clear blue and the air shimmered with the intensity of late afternoon light. Colors of autumn trees blazed all around me, each more brilliant than the next: golden, crimson, burnt orange, and mixtures I cannot describe. I marveled to myself how outstanding each and every tree was by the simple act of just being itself. Then it came, a sudden flash of recognition, a treasure of a message that has forever guided my winding, halting path.

STAND IN YOUR OWN MAGNIFICENCE!

You are sew special!

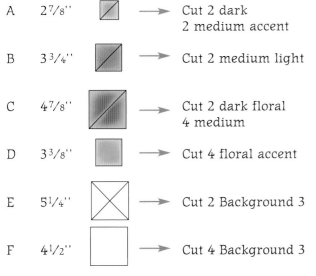

TRAVEL LOG

Here it is, our final destination. Through a lifetime of experiences, lessons, losses, and triumphs we come to discover and uncover our unparalleled selves. This voyage is an inner journey in which we unearth the rare talents, unique gifts, and singular vision we alone can share with the world. By piecing together the bits and scraps of our lives we honor our profound responsibility, that of being genuinely ourselves. We see how necessary it is to share our creative spirit, inspired by listening to our lives. Each of us stands, uniquely beautiful in our own magnificence.

Blazing Star

16'' finished

This is our last pieced block and it sits at the heart of our quilt. Use your best piecing skills to sew this as accurately as possible.

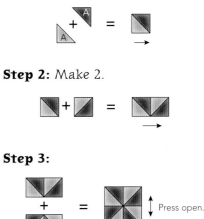

CUTTING RECIPE

A $2^7/8''$ → Cut 2 dark
2 medium accent

B $3^3/4''$ → Cut 2 medium light

C $4^7/8''$ → Cut 2 dark floral
4 medium

D $3^3/8''$ → Cut 4 floral accent

E $5^1/4''$ → Cut 2 Background 3

F $4^1/2''$ → Cut 4 Background 3

A tree is known by its fruit, a man by his deeds...

Step 1: Make 4.

Step 2: Make 2.

Step 3:

Press open.

Step 4: Mark matching marks on all B's as shown on page 17. This gives you equal bunny ears.

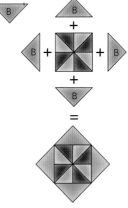

Press toward B's.

She said she was saving money for a face-lift. She was serious. Her explanation was that this would make her feel better. She was told to think of all the beautiful, joyful people she knew and to see it literally had nothing to do with waist or bottom size. She was told to wear a smile always, inside and out, to have an attitude of gratitude for all her blessings. . . all of who she was. Then she smiled and bought fabric.

Store conversation

You are the light of the world. A city on a hill cannot be hidden. Neither do people light a lamp and put it under a bowl. Instead they put it on a stand, and it gives light to everyone in the house.

Matthew 5:14-15

Step 5: Make 4.

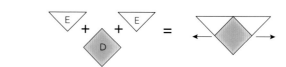

Step 6: Make 4.

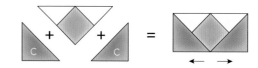

Step 7: Assemble the rows.

Rows 1 and 3

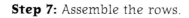

Row 2

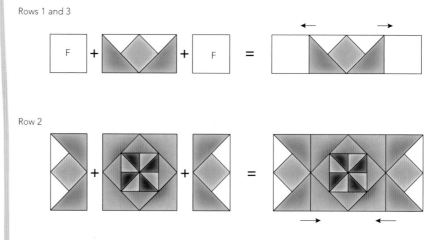

Step 8: Join the rows, carefully matching intersections. Your Blazing Star is magnificent. What a great job!

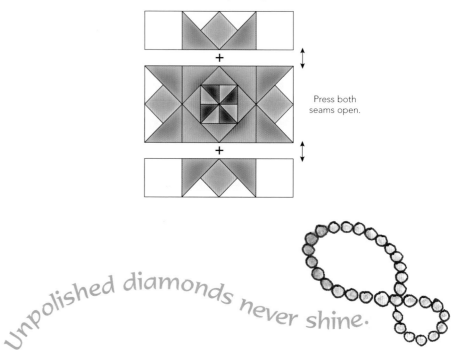

Press both seams open.

Unpolished diamonds never shine.

At Piece With Time
SETTING THE QUILT TOGETHER
Approximately 72" x 86"

Our quilt is really like an album: a photo album. It is a collection of the many adventures and memories we've had on our voyage. How exciting it is to be at the point of setting these varied parts together. This can be as creative and individual as the art of scrapbooking. Feel free to move your blocks around until they please you. The outline shown here is only a suggestion. Listen carefully to your quilt. It will tell you which blocks want to go where. Use your best quiltmaking skills to artfully stitch this masterpiece together. You will be so proud of the care and effort you take in this important final step along our path.

The blocks are set on point and are surrounded by large setting triangles. Putting the quilt together in five major sections, as illustrated, helps keep the quilt manageable. Yardage amounts are suggested, but you should always take your own personal quilt measurement across the middle of the width and length of your quilt top. Use these numbers when cutting all border fabric. Now let's get to work.

CUTTING RECIPE

BORDERS

All borders are cut to allow for mitered corners.

Border A Narrow frame surrounding center Blazing Star: Cut 4 strips $2\frac{1}{2}'' \times 20\frac{1}{2}''$.

Border B Narrow frame surrounding the pieced quilt: Cut 2 strips $2\frac{1}{2}'' \times 61''$, and 2 strips $2\frac{1}{2}'' \times 75\frac{1}{8}''$.

Border C Final large border: Cut 2 strips $6'' \times 72\frac{1}{2}''$, and 2 strips $6'' \times 86\frac{3}{8}''$.

SETTING TRIANGLES

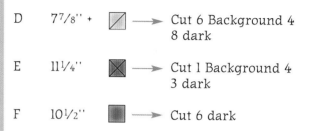

D $7\frac{7}{8}''$ +   → Cut 6 Background 4
8 dark

E $11\frac{1}{4}''$ → Cut 1 Background 4
3 dark

F $10\frac{1}{2}''$ → Cut 6 dark

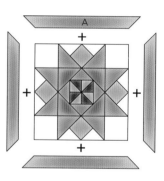

Step 1: Stitch Narrow Frame borders A to Blazing Star, mitering the corners with your favorite miter method. Press seams toward borders.

Step 2: Sew the 4 appliqué triangles to the above unit. Use your matching marks as described on page 17 to give you equal bunny ears on each triangle. Press seams toward appliqué. This is Section 1.

Section 1

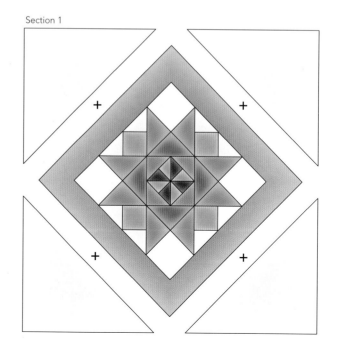

Step 3: Construct Sections 2 and 3. Press seams away from pieced blocks.

Section 2

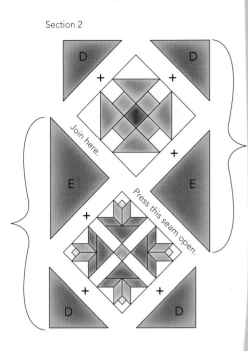

Step 4: Sew Section 2 and Section 3 to either side of Section 1. Press seams open.

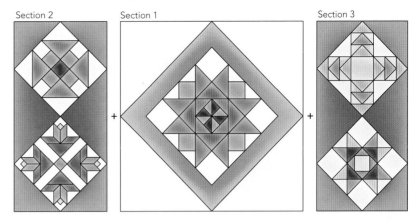

Step 5: Construct Sections 4 and 5. Sew each section into 6 diagonal rows as shown. Press seams away from pieced blocks. Now join rows to form each section. Press seams open.

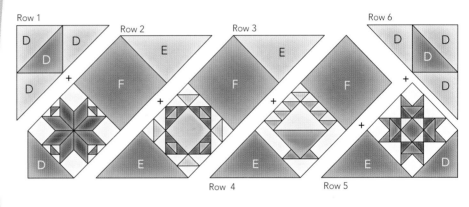

Section 3

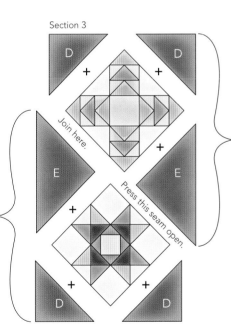

Step 6: Join Sections 4 and 5 to either side of the center section. Press seams open. Whew! What hard work! Maybe it's time for a break and something chocolate before you continue on.

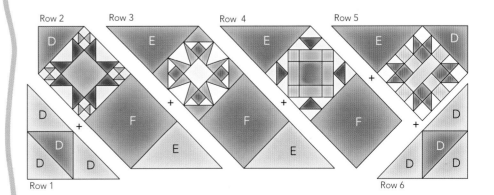

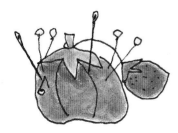

Section 4

Section 2   Section 1   +   Section 3

Section 5

I'm not going to live long
enough to finish all this stuff
I've got started. And, here
I am still starting more!
Store conversation

Step 7: Add narrow frame borders B to the quilt, mitering the corners. Press seams toward the border.

Step 8: Sew on the remaining final large borders C, mitering corners. Press seams toward borders. What an heirloom you have created!

Now the fun begins as you baste and quilt your treasure. Many of the hard decisions of color and accurate piecing are behind you. Ahead are delicious hours of embellishing the blocks with quilting. May you enjoy each and every moment!

QUILT BACKING

1. Cut your 5½-yard piece of backing fabric into 2 pieces each 2¾ yards long. Remove the selvage edges.

2. Sew these 2 pieces, right sides together along both long edges. Press seams open.

3. Cut or tear one of the backing pieces along the center of its length. You should end up with a backing that looks like this.

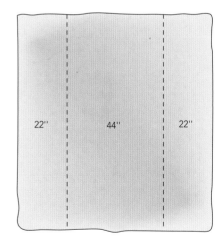

22"   44"   22"

BINDING

Cut 8 strips 2½" x 44". Seam together. Fold in half to form a double-fold straight-grain binding. Stitch to quilt. Beautiful, but remember, a quilt isn't a quilt until you've signed and dated it on the back for all future generations to admire.

Wisdom Gathered Wallhanging

32¼" X 32¼"

The "essence" of our journey is captured in this glorious wallhanging. Piece the Blazing Star and then enjoy appliquéing the surrounding triangles. It would be a stunning wallhanging on its own or a lovely accompaniment to the full-size quilt.

WHAT YOU'LL NEED

- BLAZING STAR: Fat quarters of a background fabric, a dark, a dark floral, a medium accent, a floral accent, a medium, and a medium light
- APPLIQUÉ TRIANGLES: ¾ yard second background fabric
- FAT QUARTERS OR LARGE SCRAPS: variety of reds, yellows, browns, blues and greens to form flowers, vines, leaves, acorns and nest
- FRAMING BORDERS: 1 yard for inner frame and outer frame
- BINDING: The above yardage includes enough for a 2½" double-fold straight-grain binding.
- BACKING FABRIC: 1 yard
- CRIB SIZE BATTING: 45" x 60"

Blazing Star

Follow the cutting recipe and construction directions on page 69.

APPLIQUÉD TRIANGLES

Follow the instructions for Harvest Bouquet on page 65. Note once again the use of a full square to avoid distorting the long bias edges of each triangle. This is very sturdy and allows you to stitch two appliqué triangles on one 18" square. Once the appliqué is complete, use the steps on page 66 to true up each triangle.

FRAMING BORDERS

For the inner frame, cut 4 strips 2½" x 20½". For the outer frame, cut 4 strips 2½" x 32¾".

ASSEMBLE THE WALLHANGING

Step 1: Stitch the inner frames to the Blazing Star block, mitering the corners. Press seams toward the frames.

Inner frame

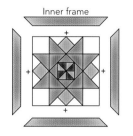

Step 2: Sew the 4 appliqué triangles to the unit created in Step 1. Use matching marks to help center each triangle and give you equal bunny ears. Press seams toward appliqué.

Step 3: Sew the outer frames to the unit created in Step 2, mitering corners. Press the seams toward the frames. Isn't it absolutely wonderful?

Outer frame

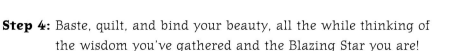

Step 4: Baste, quilt, and bind your beauty, all the while thinking of the wisdom you've gathered and the Blazing Star you are!

But where can wisdom be found? Where does understanding dwell? Man does not comprehend its worth; it cannot be found in the land of the living. The deep says, "It is not in me," the sea says, "It is not with me." It cannot be bought with the finest gold nor can its price be weighed in silver. . . the price of wisdom is beyond rubies. . . where then does wisdom come from? Where does understanding dwell? It is hidden from the eyes of every living thing, concealed even from the birds of the air. Destruction and Death say, "only a rumor of it has reached our ears." God understands the way to it and He alone knows where it dwells, for He views the ends of the earth and sees everything under the heavens. When He estab-lished the force of the wind and measured out the waters, when he made a decree for the rain and a path for the thunderstorm, then He looked at wisdom and appraised it; He confirmed it and tested it. And He said to man, "the fear of the Lord—that is wis-dom, and to shun evil is under-standing."

Job: 28

About the Authors

Kristin has been quilting for more than 25 blissful years and teaching for nearly 20. It seems she grew up with the quilt world, teaching herself at first, and then absorbing the latest techniques quiltmaking had to offer. She teaches and lectures throughout the Southeast in quilt shops, for quilt guilds, and at regional quilt symposiums where she encourages students to create from their hearts.

In 2001 she was honored to be a Resident Guest Artist at Elly Sienkiewicz's Appliqué Academy and was invited to return as a teacher in 2002, definitely a dream come true!

Kristin has her own pattern line, *Straight From My Heart Designs,* where she shares her unique design style, not quite folky but definitely not fussy, along with helpful tips for achieving beautiful appliqué.

Kristin's life in South Carolina has calmed down as her two children, Megan and Patrick, have begun lives of their own in college. There is more room to spread out her delicious fabric stash now, and more time for gardening and travel with her talented husband, Bill.

The amazing connection quilting provides is something Kristin is so proud to share. Discovering and encouraging the creativity that lies at the heart of each of us is her greatest longing.

Diane started quilting in the mid-1960s after seeing a quilt in a *Time* magazine article on folk art. She thought, "I want to make that," and did, although "poorly, with much help from store clerks, a neighbor, and my husband's aunt." That was the beginning for her, and she hasn't stopped since that first attempt. Appliqué continues to be her favorite with made-up patterns ("I can't read directions"), but she loves all the aspects of this art. She has no rules for others or herself, except to do your best.

Over the years, Diane has been amazed and blessed by work published in numerous quilting magazines, awards won, ribbons pinned on quilts, lectures given, and classes taught. She had a one-woman show in the late 1980s called *People, Places, and Quilts,* which resulted in a book of the same name published by EPM Publications.

Quite by accident she owns ("with the Lord and the bank") two quilt shops in South Carolina. Both are called *People, Places, and Quilts,* and are well run by a group of sixteen ladies who love quilting, customers, each other, and most of the time, Diane. One is in Summerville (which was honored to be selected as one of the top ten quilt shops in North America for the year 2000), and more recently, one in Charleston.

Diane lives happily in Summerville, South Carolina, and loves all that is "good, right, and holy: people, animals, community, church, workplace and workmates, gardening, sewing, reading, drawing, writing, the outdoors, four grown children, one daughter-in-law, and a mom who right now is saying, 'Oh Di, did you have to go and say all that?' Well, yes!"

Kristin and Diane co-authored

A Southern Album. . .a Quilt Celebrating Southern Culture, History and Hopes

(available through People, Places, and Quilts Press www.ppquilts.com).

A Fond Farewell

As we come to the end of our time together, I would rather say see you later than goodbye. I'll see you at the quilt store, choosing the perfect thread to stitch your quilt. I'll be at a quilt bee or with your closest friends when you discuss the meaning of growing into womanhood. I'll look for the twinkle in your eye as you tell admirers the stories about your quilt designs. I'll catch my breath when I see you glowing with radiance at a quilt show. I will see you later, for our journey is just beginning. May we be strong, may we be our truest selves, may we be at peace with time.

With all my love, Kristi

Well, it is the end of this book but the start of something else for you I hope. . . forward march and march forward. . . into the promised land. . . Canaan. This watercolor and ink illustration is a gift for you to frame or leave in the book. Look closely, everything is there: the quilt, all the block symbols, cooked cake, baby doll and quilt, children, Kristi and me, pets, young man on the bench, and more. Seek and ye shall find, literally and figuratively!

Blessings and Amen, Diane

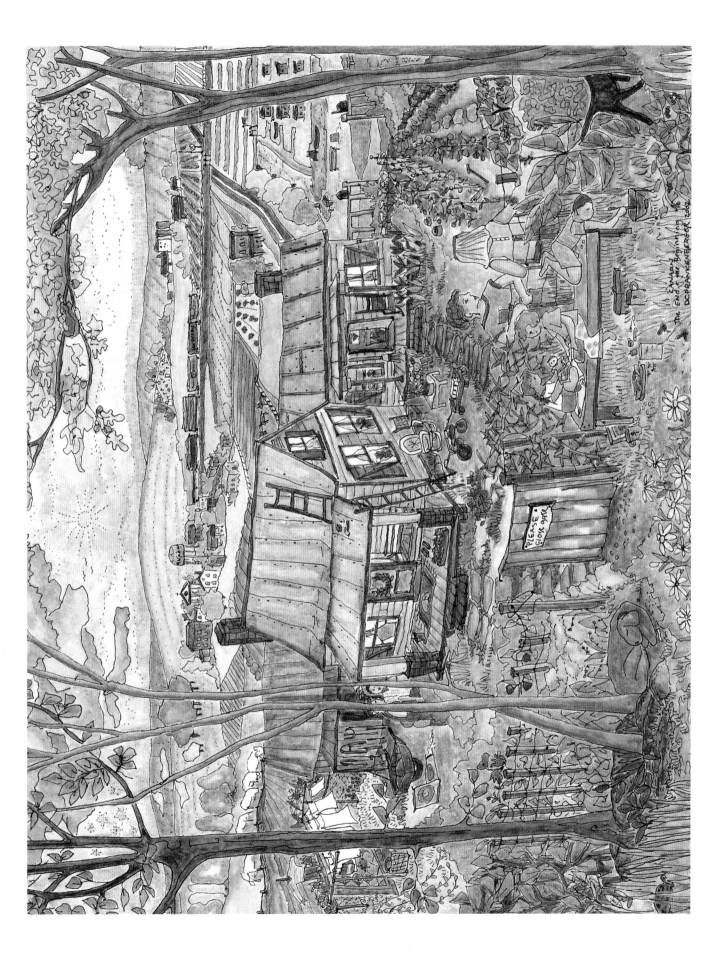

Illumination For The Journey
BIBLIOGRAPHY

I adore books! I love the gift of words from those who write well and think hard. Here are a few of my favorites.

Resources for Patchwork Patterns

Beyer, Jinny, *The Quilter's Album of Blocks and Borders*, EPM Publications, 1980.

Brackman, Barbara, *Encyclopedia, of Pieced Quilt Patterns*, AQS, 1993.

McCloskey, Marsha, *Block Party*, Rodale, 1998.

Resources for Symbols and Their Meanings

Greenaway, Kate, *Language of Flowers*, Dover, 1992.

Tresidder, Jack, *Dictionary of Symbols*, Chronicle Books, 1997.

Sienkiewicz, Elly, *Spoken Without a Word*, Self-published.

Resources for Creativity

Bayles, David and Ted Orland, *Art and Fear*, Capra Press, Santa Barbara, CA, 1993.

Cameron, Julia, *The Artist's Way*, G. P. Putnam's Sons, New York, NY, 1992.

Messer, Mari, *Pencil Dancing*, Walking Stick Press, Cincinatti, OH, 2001.

Phillips, Jan, *Marry Your Muse*, Quest Books. Theosophical Publishing House, Wheaton, IL, 1997

Other fine books from C&T Publishing

24 Quilted Gems: Sparkling Traditional & Original Projects, Gai Perry

All About Quilting from A to Z, From the Editors and Contributors of *Quilter's Newsletter Magazine* and *Quiltmaker* magazine

Appliqué 12 Easy Ways!: Charming Quilts, Giftable Projects, & Timeless Techniques, Elly Sienkiewicz

Appliqué Inside the Lines: 12 Quilt Projects to Embroider & Appliqué, Carol Armstrong

Art of Classic Quiltmaking, The, Harriet Hargrave & Sharyn Craig

Baltimore Beauties and Beyond Vol. I: Studies In Classic Album Quilt Appliqué, Elly Sienkiewicz

Beautifully Quilted with Alex Anderson: • *How to Choose or Create the Best Designs for Your Quilt* • *6 Timeless Projects* • *Full-Size Patterns, Ready to Use*, Alex Anderson

Best of Baltimore Beauties, The: 95 Patterns for Album Blocks and Borders, Elly Sienkiewicz

Best of Baltimore Beauties Part II, The: More Patterns for Album Blocks, Elly Sienkiewicz

Block Magic, Too!: Over 50 NEW Blocks from Squares and Rectangles, Nancy Johnson-Srebro

Cats in Quilts: 14 Purrfect Projects, Carol Armstrong

Celebrate the Tradition with C&T Publishing: Over 70 Fabulous New Blocks, Tips & Stories from Quilting's Best, C&T Staff

Dresden Flower Garden: A New Twist on Two Quilt Classics, Blanche Young

Elm Creek Quilts: Quilt Projects Inspired by the Elm Creek Quilts Novels, Jennifer Chiaverini & Nancy Odom

Fancy Appliqué: 12 Lessons to Enhance Your Skills, Elly Sienkiewicz

Fantastic Fans: Exquisite Quilts & Other Projects, Alice Dunsdon

Fast, Fun & Easy Fabric Bowls: 5 Reversible Shapes to Use & Display, Linda Johanson

Felt Wee Folk: Enchanting Projects, Salley Mavor

Floral Affair, A: Quilts & Accessories for Romantics, Nihon Vogue

Flowering Favorites from Piece O' Cake Designs: Becky Goldsmith & Linda Jenkins

Hand Appliqué with Alex Anderson: Seven Projects for Hand Appliqué, Alex Anderson

Hunter Star Quilts & Beyond: Jan Krentz

Liberated String Quilts, Gwen Marston

Make it Simpler Paper Piecing: • *No Pins!* • *Pieced on One Sheet!* • *Fold 'n Sew Technique!*, Anita Grossman Solomon

Mastering Machine Appliqué, 2nd Edition: The Complete Guide Including: • *Invisible Machine Appliqué* • *Satin Stitch* • *Blanket Stitch & Much More*, Harriet Hargrave

New Look at Log Cabin Quilts, A: Design a Scene Block by Block PLUS 10 Easy-to-Follow Projects, Flavin Glover

Perfect Union of Patchwork & Appliqué, A, Darlene Christopherson

Plentiful Possibilities: A Timeless Treasury of 16 Terrific Quilts, Lynda Milligan & Nancy Smith

Quick-Strip Paper Piecing: For Blocks, Borders & Quilts, Peggy Martin

Radiant New York Beauties: 14 Paper-Pieced Quilt Projects, Valori Wells

Reverse Appliqué with No Brakez, Jan Mullen

Ricky Tims' Convergence Quilts: Mysterious, Magical, Easy, and Fun, Ricky Tims

Shoreline Quilts: 15 Glorious Get-Away Projects, compiled by Cyndy Rymer

Show Me How to Machine Quilt: A Fun, No-Mark Approach, Kathy Sandbach

Simple Fabric Folding for Christmas: 14 Festive Quilts & Projects, Liz Aneloski

Sweet Dreams, Moon Baby: A Quilt to Make, A Story to Read, Elly Sienkiewicz

Teddy Bear Redwork: • *25 Fresh, New Designs* • *Step-by-Step Projects* • *Quilts and More*, Jan Rapacz

Totally Tubular Quilts: A New Strip-Piecing Technique, Rita Hutchens

Wine Country Quilts: A Bounty of Flavorful Projects for Any Palette, Cyndy Lyle Rymer & Jennifer Rounds

When Quilters Gather: 20 Patterns of Piecers at Play, Ruth McDowell

For more information, ask for a free catalog:
C&T Publishing, Inc.
P.O. Box 1456
Lafayette, CA 94549
(800) 284-1114
Email: ctinfo@ctpub.com
Website: www.ctpub.com

For quilting supplies:
Cotton Patch Mail Order
3405 Hall Lane, Dept.CTB
Lafayette, CA 94549
(800) 835-4418
(925) 283-7883
Email:quiltusa@yahoo.com
Website: www.quiltusa.com

Note: Fabrics used in the quilts shown may not be currently available since fabric manufacturers keep most fabrics in print for only a short time.